Latin

TWO

FOR COMMON ENTRANCE

N. R. R. Oulton

About the author

Nicholas Oulton read History at Oriel College, Oxford and has an MA in Classics from London University. He taught Latin and Greek for ten years before writing the *So you really want to learn Latin* course and founding Galore Park in 1998.

Acknowledgements

The author and the publisher would like to thank Stephen Anderson for his generosity and support in producing this book. Stephen studied classics at Trinity College, Dublin and St John's College, Cambridge. From 1980 to 2015 he taught at Winchester College, where he was Head of Classics from 1984 to 2008 and subsequently Senior Tutor. In October 2015 he took up a new post as Lecturer in Classical Languages at New College, Oxford.

The publishers would like to thank the following for permission to reproduce copyright material:

Photo credits p7 © Leemage/UIG via Getty Images **p10** © The Art Archive / Alamy Stock Photo **p16** © The Art Archive / Alamy Stock Photo **p23** © Iberfoto/SuperStock **p33** © bilwissedition Ltd. & Co. KG / Alamy Stock Photo **p45** © Robert Preston Photography / Alamy Stock Photo **p68** © Photos.com/Getty Images/Thinkstock **p77** © DEA PICTURE LIBRARY/De Agostini/Getty Images **p85** © North Wind Picture Archives / Alamy Stock Photo **p97** © The Art Archive / Alamy Stock Photo

Every effort has been made to trace all copyright holders, but if any have been inadvertently overlooked, the publishers will be pleased to make the necessary arrangements at the first opportunity.

Although every effort has been made to ensure that website addresses are correct at time of going to press, Galore Park cannot be held responsible for the content of any website mentioned in this book. It is sometimes possible to find a relocated web page by typing in the address of the home page for a website in the URL window of your browser.

Hachette UK's policy is to use papers that are natural, renewable and recyclable products and made from wood grown in sustainable forests. The logging and manufacturing processes are expected to conform to the environmental regulations of the country of origin.

Orders: please contact Bookpoint Ltd, 130 Park Drive, Milton Park, Abingdon, Oxon OX14 4SE. Telephone: (44) 01235 827720. Fax: (44) 01235 400454. Email education@bookpoint.co.uk Lines are open from 9 a.m. to 5 p.m., Monday to Saturday, with a 24-hour message answering service. Visit our website at www.galorepark.co.uk for details of other revision guides for Common Entrance, examination papers and Galore Park publications.

ISBN: 9781471867415

Text copyright © N.R.R. Oulton 2016

First published in 2016 by

Galore Park Publishing Ltd,

An Hachette UK Company

Carmelite House

50 Victoria Embankment

London EC4Y 0DZ

www.galorepark.co.uk

Impression number   10 9 8 7 6 5

Year   2020

Cover photo © AskinTulayOver - istockphoto.com

Illustration of a Roman soldier on p31 by Tony Randall. All other illustrations by Aptara, Inc.

Typeset in India

Printed in India

A catalogue record for this title is available from the British Library.

Contents

Contents

iv

Introduction

In this book we dig deeper into the workings of the Latin language, learning to cope with 3rd declension nouns and adjectives, two more tenses and a whole load of irregular verbs. Just as importantly, we learn more about the Romans themselves: their food and clothing, their houses and their leisure pastimes, and more of their history, including a sneak preview of the mighty Julius Caesar. We also read stories about Ulysses (better known to most of us as Odysseus) on his way home from the Trojan War, and Perseus, the slayer of the Gorgon Medusa.

The Romans, as you may know by now, were fascinated by the culture of Ancient Greece, and absorbed much of it into their own. Be careful, however, with the fact that in many cases, they gave Latin names to Greek gods, goddesses and figures from mythology. Thus we read in Latin of the hero Ulixēs, translated into English as Ulysses, but known to the Greeks as Odysseus. A similar thing happens with the king of the gods. The Romans called him Iuppiter, translated into English as Jupiter, and known to the Greeks as Zeus.

As in Book 1, we have marked the vowels on the Latin words where these should be pronounced as long with a macron (e.g. nārrat, fēmina, īnsula, rogō, tūtus). Learning to pronounce the words correctly is an important part of Latin. As you go further with the language, and start reading Latin poetry, you will find it essential to know whether a vowel is long or short, and the best way to master this is to learn it correctly when you first meet a new word.

Once again, vocabularies for learning are given at the end of each chapter, and a complete set of English–Latin and Latin–English vocabularies is given at the end of the book. There is a summary of all the grammar that you cover in Books 1 and 2 at the back, and you will also find there a more detailed guide to pronunciation.

◯ Notes on features in this book

⟨ Exercise ⟩ ─────────────────────────

Exercises are provided to give you plenty of opportunities to practise what you have learned.

> Useful rules and reminders are scattered throughout the book.

The box on the right makes it clear that you are studying a non-linguistic topic required by the ISEB Classics syllabus. Non-linguistic topics are about:

> This topic is part of the Non-Linguistic Studies section of the ISEB syllabus.

- aspects of domestic life in Rome
- early Roman legends
- Roman entertainment
- the Roman army
- Roman Britain
- Greek mythology.

There is a wealth of information to help you with the questions in these non-linguistic topics in *Greeks & Romans* by A.M. Wright, published by Galore Park.

Go further ─────────────────────────

This heading highlights material that is beyond the requirements of the ISEB syllabus. You do not need to remember this material for your exam, but it will help you understand some interesting aspects of the language.

1 3rd declension nouns

Nouns of the 3rd declension have a genitive singular ending in -is and decline like rēx:

rēx, rēg-is, m. = king		
	Singular	Plural
Nominative	rēx	rēg-ēs
Vocative	rēx	rēg-ēs
Accusative	rēg-em	rēg-ēs
Genitive	rēg-is	rēg-um
Dative	rēg-ī	rēg-ibus
Ablative	rēg-e	rēg-ibus

Masculine and feminine nouns decline like rēx. So do common nouns (i.e. ones that could be either masculine or feminine, such as comes = a companion). The secret to success when using 3rd declension nouns is getting the **STEM** right. You should be used to working with stems by now, but in the 3rd declension there is often a dramatic and totally unpredictable change in the stem. Thus, whereas puella (1st declension) has the perfectly reasonable stem of puell-, and dominus (2nd declension) has the stem domin-, the 3rd declension noun rēx has a stem of rēg-, and mīles has the stem mīlit-.

What this means is that when you meet a 3rd declension noun for the first time, you need to find out its genitive singular, and thus (by chopping off the -is) its stem. Then you add the **ENDINGS** above to that stem, and everything works normally. But without the stem, you are lost.

Exercise 1.1

Study the information above about 3rd declension nouns like rēx. Notice how, once you have got past the vocative singular, the endings are added to the stem (which is found in the genitive singular, by chopping off -is). Write out in full:

1 clāmor, clāmōr-is, m. = shout

2 uxor, uxōr-is, f. = wife

3 dux, duc-is, c. = leader

Exercise 1.2

Here are some more 3rd declension nouns:

comes, comitis, c. = companion

coniūnx, coniugis, c. = husband, wife

homō, hominis, m. = man

lūx, lūcis, f. = light

mīles, mīlitis, m. = soldier

parēns, parentis, c. = parent

Using these, and the ones above, translate into Latin:

1 Of the companion

2 Towards the wives

3 Of the men

4 Out of the light

5 O parents!

6 With the wife

7 The kings (nom.)

8 The kings (acc.)

9 By a shout

10 With the soldiers

Exercise 1.3

Translate into English:

1 rēgis

2 comitis

3 cum coniugibus

4 hominum

5 in lūcem

6 contrā mīlitem

7 dē parentibus

8 clāmōrēs

9 uxōrī

10 prope ducem

◯ Working with 3rd declension nouns

Extra care needs to be taken when translating sentences with 3rd declension nouns, because the nominative and accusative plural endings are the same.

E.g. mīlitēs comitēs laudant = The soldiers praise their companions.

In some sentences, you may have to use your common sense to work out what it means.

E.g.   ducēs spectābant = The leaders were watching.

OR

They were watching the leaders.

Finally, note that you must be careful not to muddle up the endings of 1st or 2nd declension nouns that you have already learnt with the new 3rd declension endings that you are learning now. Some of the same endings (-is, -i, -e, -um) occur, but for different cases, and could potentially be confused if you don't know which declension the noun is.

E.g. puer**ī** rēg**ī** cantant = The boys are singing to the king.

E.g. oppid**um** duc**um** oppugnāmus = We are attacking the town of the leaders.

But if you follow the rules of translation carefully (look at the VERB FIRST!), and learn your vocabulary thoroughly, you should be safe.

Exercise 1.4

Translate into English:

1 clāmōrēs fēminārum audīvimus.

2 rēx comitēs numquam superāvit.

3 dux coniugem mīlitis spectābat.

4 Rōmānī mulierēs in oppidum dūxērunt.

5 mīles lūcem uxōrī ostendit.

6 puella cibum parentibus dedit.

7 servī uxōrem rēgis timēbant.

8 nūntiī clāmōrēs comitum audīvērunt.

9 vir cum coniuge habitāre amat.

10 lūx in caelō aderat.

Neuter 3rd declension nouns

Neuter 3rd declension nouns behave as you might expect. That is to say, just as the neuter noun bellum has identical endings in the nominative, vocative and accusative cases, so it is with 3rd declension nouns. Thus corpus behaves as follows:

corpus, corpor-is, n. = body	Singular	Plural
Nominative	corpus	corpor-a
Vocative	corpus	corpor-a
Accusative	corpus	corpor-a
Genitive	corpor-is	corpor-um
Dative	corpor-ī	corpor-ibus
Ablative	corpor-e	corpor-ibus

As with nouns like rēx, the key to success with these nouns is getting the stem right. For the first three cases in the singular, the word remains unchanged. Then, for all cases after the accusative singular, the endings above are added to the stem, and are very similar to the endings for rēx.

Another thing to look out for is that neuter nouns in -us look rather as if they should go like dominus. The genitive singular, however, should make it clear that they are 3rd declension.

Exercise 1.5

Study the information above about 3rd declension neuter nouns like corpus. Notice how, once you have got past the nominative, vocative and accusative singular, the endings are added to the stem (which is found in the genitive singular). Write out in full:

1 flūmen, flūminis, n. = river

2 iter, itineris, n. = journey

3 nōmen, nōminis, n. = name

◯ Agreement of adjectives with 3rd declension nouns

Care needs to be taken when making an adjective such as bonus agree with a 3rd declension noun. Nothing strange happens, but you may *feel* something strange is happening because the two words stand almost no chance of rhyming. Gone are the happy days of puella bona, or dominus bonus. Now we have to put up with rēx bonus (masculine), uxor bona (feminine) and corpus bonum (neuter). We have met this sort of thing before, with bonus not rhyming with masculine nouns such as agricola, so it shouldn't cause you too much trouble. Stick to the rules of adjective agreement and you will be fine.

> **nōmine = by name**
>
> The best way of translating the English word *called* (as in 'a boy called Marcus') is to use the ablative singular of nōmen = name.
>
> E.g. A boy called Marcus = puer nōmine Mārcus (i.e. a boy *by name* Marcus).

Exercise 1.6

Study the information above about the agreement of adjectives with 3rd declension nouns. Remember, adjective agreement has nothing to do with rhyming. When it rhymes, it's a bonus. So, just work out which case and gender the noun is and then put the adjective into that form.

Translate into Latin:

1 The good kings (nom.)

2 Depart, bad king!

3 The tired soldier (acc.)

4 Of the small river

5 For the new body

6 With a good leader

7 Towards the big river

8 The long journeys (nom.)

9 With our soldiers

10 The wife of the angry leader

Exercise 1.7

Translate into English:

1 in flūmen altum

2 in flūmine altō

3 prope corpus magnum

4 contrā mīlitēs fessōs

5 cum rēge malō

6 coniunx mea cantat.

7 uxōrēs pulchrās spectātis.

8 rēx, Rōmulus nōmine

9 clāmōrēs magnās audīvī.

10 per lūcem clāram

Exercise 1.8

Study the information above about the use of nōmine = by name. Then translate into English:

1 rēx malus, nōmine Tarquinius, Rōmānōs diū terrēbat.

2 puella, nōmine Lucrētia, fīlium saevum rēgis timēbat.

3 mīlitēs Brūtī Tarquinium ex urbe discēdere cupiēbant.

4 Tarquinius Superbus ā rēge nōmine Porsennā auxilium rogāvit.

5 Porsenna multīs cum mīlitibus ad flūmen festīnāvit.

6 'urbemne nostram' inquit Brūtus 'servāre cupitis?'

7 'hostēs saevōs' inquit Horātius 'ego superāre cupiō.'

8 mīles validus cum comitibus Rōmānīs urbem fortiter dēfendit.

9 rēx saevus mīlitēs Rōmānōs diū spectābat.

10 tandem rēx nōmine Porsenna ā flūmine discessit.

A note on names

The Romans greatly admired the art and literature of the Greeks, and much of their own culture was heavily dependent on that of Greece.

One thing to watch out for, though, is that there are often Roman names for Greek gods and goddesses, and for famous figures in Greek literature.

A good example of this is the hero Ulysses. Ulysses (in Latin, Ulixēs) is the name given by the Romans to the Greek hero Odysseus, whose adventures are told by Homer in his epic poem *The Odyssey*.

Another important area where names are different is the gods and goddesses. Here is a table showing the gods of Mount Olympus and how these differ between Greek and Roman:

Greek	Roman	Role
Zeus	Jupiter	King of the gods
Hera	Juno	His wife; goddess of women
Aphrodite	Venus	The goddess of love
Athena	Minerva	Goddess of wisdom
Hephaestos	Vulcan	The blacksmith god
Hades	Pluto	The god of the Underworld
Hermes	Mercury	The messenger god
Poseidon	Neptune	God of the sea
Demeter	Ceres	Goddess of agriculture
Apollo	Apollo	God of prophecy, music and the arts
Ares	Mars	God of war
Hestia	Vesta	Goddess of the hearth
Dionysos	Bacchus	God of wine
Artemis	Diana	Goddess of hunting

Exercise 1.9

Translate into English:

Ulysses and the bag of winds

Ulixēs, ubi Graecī urbem Troiam <u>expugnāvērunt</u>, cum comitibus ad īnsulam
Aeōliam nāvigāvit. in īnsulā habitābat Aeōlus, rēx ventōrum. diū cum rēge
Ulixēs et comitēs manēbant. tandem, ubi Graecī discēdere cupiēbant,
Aeōlus ventum <u>Zephyrum</u> <u>ēmīsit</u>; <u>relīquōs</u> tamen ventōs īn* <u>saccō</u> tenuit.
5 <u>saccum</u> ducī clārō dedit et dē ventīs monuit. 'tenē <u>saccum</u>' inquit 'et ad
patriam cum comitibus tuīs nāvigā. ventus <u>Zephyrus</u> semper ad <u>Ithacam</u>
dūcit.'
    ubi ad patriam veniēbant, Ulixēs, quod fessus erat, dormiēbat. comitēs
tamen nōn dormiēbant. comitēs <u>saccum</u> ducis spectābant et 'cūr <u>saccum</u>
10 semper tenet?' inquiunt. 'quid īn <u>saccō</u> tenet Ulixēs?'
    ūnus ē comitibus ad ducem appropinquāvit et <u>saccum</u> cēpit. 'aurum īn <u>saccō</u>
portat!' inquit. 'aurum ducī nostrō rēx Aeōlus dedit!'
    comitēs īrātī erant et <u>saccum</u> <u>aperuērunt</u>. statim ventī ē <u>saccō</u> ruērunt et
nāvem ad īnsulam Aeōliam <u>reppulērunt</u>. frūstrā Ulixēs et comitēs auxilium ā
15 rēge rogāvērunt. 'Ulixēs <u>inimīcus</u> deōrum est' inquit rēx. itaque Graecī in
nāvem festīnāvērunt et ab īnsulā discessērunt. ventus tamen nōn iam ad
patriam dūcēbat.

* Remember, a vowel is always pronounced as long if it is followed by ns or nf, even if
these letters are spread across two words, as in a phrase such as <u>īn</u> <u>s</u>accō.

■ Ulysses and the bag of winds – an artist's impression

expugnō, -āre = I take by storm
Zephyrus, -ī, m. = the westerly wind
ēmittō, -ere, ēmīsī = I let loose
relīquus, -a, -um = the remaining, other
saccus, -ī, m. = bag
Ithaca, -ae, f. = Ithaca (the home of Ulysses)
aperiō, -īre, aperuī = I open
repellō, -ere, reppulī = I drive back
inimīcus, -ī, m. = an enemy

Go further

One of the great skills when translating from Latin, as from any language, is to write English which is natural. Try not to do a word-for-word translation, which may show that you know what the individual words mean but does not show that you can convert the Latin into real English.

For example, in the passage above, consider the sentence:

ubi ad patriam veniēbant, Ulixēs, quod fessus erat, dormiēbat.

You may have been tempted to translate this as 'When they were coming to the fatherland, Ulysses, because he was tired, was sleeping.'

While this may be what the individual words mean, this does not sound at all natural. First, we can do much better than that with regard to the English word order. But even more importantly, we can think about how best to translate the phrase ubi ad patriam veniēbant, and the verb dormiēbat. For example, how about 'When they were drawing close to their fatherland' rather than 'when they were coming to the fatherland'? And for dormiēbat, how about 'he fell asleep' or 'he went to sleep' rather than 'he was sleeping'?

The secret to this is to translate the Latin literally first, being sure you have understood what it means, and then put that into good, natural English.

◯ English derivations

You should be pretty good by now at finding the link between Latin and English words. With English words that come from 3rd declension nouns, you will see that very often the word comes from the noun stem, rather than the nominative form. Your spelling will improve enormously once you get used to this.

Thus:

itin**ine**rary from iter, it**ine**ris

mil**i**tary from mīles, mīlitis

nom**i**nate from nomen, nominis

Exercise 1.10

Explain the connection between the following Latin and English words:

1 rēgem   regal
2 coniugis   conjugal
3 itineris   itinerary
4 urbem   urban
5 mīlitēs   military

6 nāvem   navy
7 frūstrā   frustrate
8 mānsērunt   mansion
9 patriam   patriotic
10 īrātī   irate

Vocabulary 1

Latin	English
clāmor, clāmōris, m.	shout
comes, comitis, c.	companion
coniūnx, coniugis, c.	husband, wife
corpus, corporis, n.	body
dux, ducis, m.	leader
flūmen, flūminis, n.	river
homō, hominis, m.	man, woman
iter, itineris, n.	journey
lūx, lūcis, f.	light
mīles, mīlitis, m.	soldier
mulier, mulieris, f.	woman
nōmen, nōminis, n.	name
parēns, parentis, c.	parent
rēx, rēgis, m.	king
uxor, uxōris, f.	wife

Food and meals

It is likely that when Ulysses stayed with Aeolus, the king of the winds, he would have been entertained to a series of rich feasts. The Romans loved their food, and much of what they would have eaten is what one might expect to eat in a Mediterranean country today.

This topic is part of the Non-Linguistic Studies section of the ISEB syllabus.

A typical day's menus might have looked like this:

iēntāculum (breakfast)
Bread, fruit, olives and honey, washed down with water or wine

prandium (lunch)
Bread, fruit, cheese, olives and dried figs

cēna (dinner)
Consisting of three courses: gustātiō (starter), prīmae mēnsae (main course) and secundae mēnsae (dessert)

(For this one would expect to have eaten plenty of fish and vegetables. Special delicacies included stuffed dormice (glīrēs), oysters, lampreys, boar and peacock)

■ Mosaic of a Roman dinner party – from Carthage, in modern-day Tunisia

If one were going to a dinner, it would have been held in the triclīnium (dining room), with the diners typically reclining on three couches around a table or tables on which the food was arranged. The food would have been brought in by slaves, and a considerable quantity of wine would have been drunk. Hosts often liked to show off their wealth by throwing extravagant parties with exotic dishes, such as wild boar accompanied by sucking piglets, hog stuffed with sausages and meat puddings, chicken served with pastry-capped goose eggs, oysters, scallops and snails. During the dinner, the entertainment might consist of actors and acrobats performing for the guests, as well as poetry reading and elevated conversation.

There is a famous account of a dinner party thrown by a rich Roman glutton called Trimalchio in which at least twelve courses were served, each more exotic than the one before. Although this account is an exaggerated, comic view of someone showing off and pretending to be grander than he really was, it gives a vivid view of how life in Ancient Rome might have been for those with money enough to enjoy it.

Exercise 1.11

(a) (i) Write a shopping list for a day's meals at home, saying which food items are for which meal.

   (ii) Give two ways in which this list might be different from a list you might write today.

(b) (i) You have been invited to a dinner party in Ancient Rome. Describe the occasion, including what you expect to eat and how the food will be served.

   (ii) Give two ways in which the occasion would be different from a modern dinner party.

(c) (i) Tell the story of how King Aeolus tried to help Odysseus* on his return to Ithaca after the Trojan War.

   (ii) Do you think the story would have had a different ending had Odysseus told his companions about the bag of winds?

(d) (i) List the gods of Mount Olympus, giving both their Greek names and their Roman ones.

   (ii) Which two of these would you most like to have had looking after you, and why?

*Remember that Odysseus is the hero whom the Romans called Ulysses.

2 The future tense; non-increasing 3rd declension nouns

◯ The future tense

We have learnt how to say what is happening now (using the present tense), or what happened in the past (using the imperfect and perfect tenses). We will now learn how to say what will happen in the future.

The first two conjugations use the same endings for the future tense, as follows:

1st person singular	amā-bō	I shall love
2nd person singular	amā-bis	You will love
3rd person singular	amā-bit	He/she/it will love
1st person plural	amā-bimus	We shall love
2nd person plural	amā-bitis	You will love
3rd person plural	amā-bunt	They will love
1st person singular	monē-bō	I shall warn
2nd person singular	monē-bis	You will warn
3rd person singular	monē-bit	He/she/it will warn
1st person plural	monē-bimus	We shall warn
2nd person plural	monē-bitis	You will warn
3rd person plural	monē-bunt	They will warn

Exercise 2.1

Study the information above about the future tense. Notice how the endings are added to the present stem of the verb. Notice also how the word *shall* should really be used instead of *will* in the 1st person, although this may sound a little old-fashioned. Translate into English:

1 festīnābunt.

2 labōrābis.

3 terrēbimus.

4 amābitis.

5 vocābit.

6 manēbunt.

7 nāvigābis.

8 dēlēbunt.

9 timēbō.

10 iubēbitis.

Exercise 2.2

Translate into Latin:

1 I shall build.

2 They will have.

3 You (sing.) will sing.

4 He will destroy.

5 She will hurry.

6 We shall laugh.

7 You (pl.) will have.

8 They will call.

9 You (pl.) will work.

10 We shall see.

Exercise 2.3

Translate into English:

1 dabit.

2 habitābis.

3 intrābunt.

4 laudābō.

5 necābitis.

6 oppugnābimus.

7 portābō.

8 rogābunt.

9 stābis.

10 habēbimus.

11 monēbis.

12 movēbitis.

13 rīdēbunt.

14 timēbō.

15 vidēbis.

16 dēlēbunt.

17 iubēbō.

18 respondēbunt.

19 tenēbit.

20 terrēbimus.

⬤ Non-increasing 3rd declension nouns

Most 3rd declension nouns have (at least) one more syllable in their genitive singular than in their nominative singular, and are thus said to be *increasing*.

E.g.   rēx (1 syllable);   rēgis (2 syllables)

         mīles (2 syllables);   mīlitis (3 syllables)

         iter (2 syllables);   itineris (4 syllables)

But there is a class of 3rd declension nouns which does not do this and is thus called *non-increasing*.

E.g.   cīvis (2 syllables);   cīvis (2 syllables)

         mare (2 syllables);   maris (2 syllables)

Masculine and feminine non-increasing nouns decline like cīvis, cīvis, c. = citizen. Neuter ones decline like mare, maris, n. = sea. The endings to watch out for are shown in bold.

Nom.	cīvis	mare
Voc.	cīvis	mare
Acc.	cīv-em	mare
Gen.	cīv-is	mar-is
Dat.	cīv-ī	mar-ī
Abl.	cīv-e	mar-ī
Nom.	cīv-ēs	mar-ia
Voc.	cīv-ēs	mar-ia
Acc.	cīv-ēs	mar-ia
Gen.	cīv-ium	mar-ium
Dat.	cīv-ibus	mar-ibus
Abl.	cīv-ibus	mar-ibus

Common exceptions

There are some nouns which *increase* but which take their endings from cīvis and mare, and there are some which do *not* increase, but which take their endings from rēx and corpus.

1 The following non-increasing nouns go like rēx (i.e. they go -um in the genitive plural):
   senex (old man), iuvenis (young man), pater (father), māter (mother), frāter (brother).

These are easy to remember because they are all members of the family.

2 Monosyllables which have a stem ending in two consonants go like cīvis (i.e. they go -ium in the genitive plural):
E.g. urbs, u<u>rb</u>-is, f. = city; mōns, mo<u>nt</u>-is, m. = mountain.

Exercise 2.4

Translate into English:

1 rēx Rōmānōrum cīvēs monuit.

2 mīlitēs ducem ad mare dūxērunt.

3 Rōmulus urbem magnam aedificābit.

4 mīlitēs urbem hostium oppugnābunt.

5 mīlitēs prope urbem superāvimus.

6 senex Rōmānōs dē hostibus monuit.

7 mulier parentēs coniugis nōn amābat.

8 iuvenis maria patriae vidēre cupiēbat.

9 nautae nāvem ad īnsulam nāvigābunt.

10 Ulixēs per multās terrās et maria alta errābat.

Exercise 2.5

Translate the following into Latin:

1 Kings did not rule in the city of the Romans.

2 The soldiers will wait for the famous leader.

3 We shall attack the city with many arrows.

4 Why has the leader warned the soldiers?

5 The Romans will watch the leader of the city.

6 We shall carry the food and wine to the temple of the citizens.

7 We made long journeys through seas and high mountains.

8 I was playing in the river with the young man.

9 The young man loved his dear wife.

10 The old men will wander through the high mountains.

Study the following passage and answer the questions on the opposite page.

Ulysses and the enchantress Circe

    Ulixēs cum comitibus ōlim ad īnsulam <u>Aeaeam</u> nāvigāvit. in īnsulā
habitābat Circe, dea propter <u>artem</u> <u>magicam</u> nōta. Ulixēs, ubi ad īnsulam
advēnit, prope mare, prope nāvem manēbat. <u>aliōs</u> comitēs manēre, <u>aliōs</u>
cum Eurylochō, virō validō et nōtō, aquam petere iussit. Eurylochō et
5 comitibus 'festīnāte!' inquit Ulixes. 'aquam et cibum invenīte et ad
nāvem portāte!'

    Eurylochus et comitēs in partem <u>interiōrem</u> īnsulae festīnāvērunt et mox
magnam <u>domum</u> in mediā <u>silvā</u>* vīdērunt. prope <u>domum</u> multa <u>animālia</u>
errābant. tum dea pulchra ad Graecōs appropinquāvit et cibum dedit. laetī
10 erant et deam laudāvērunt. Eurylochus sōlus deam timēbat <u>nec</u> in <u>domum</u>
deae intrāvit. subitō dea saeva virōs <u>virgā</u> <u>percussit</u> et īn <u>suēs</u> <u>vertit</u>.
Eurylochus fūgit et tūtus ad relīquōs Graecōs vēnit. ibi ducī <u>fābulam</u> dē
perīculō comitum nārrāvit.

    Ulixēs perterritus erat sed in partem <u>interiōrem</u> īnsulae festīnāvit. 'comitēs
15 nostrōs servābō!' inquit.

* See note on *In the middle on the opposite page.*

■ Ulysses' men turned into pigs by Circe – from a classical
Greek oil flask

Aeaea, -ae, f. = Aeaea
(an island)
ars, artis, f. = art, skill
magicus, -a, -um = magic
aliī ... aliī = some ... others
interiōrem (acc.) = the
interior (adjective)
domum (acc. f.) = house
silva, -ae, f. = wood
animal, animālis, n. = animal
virga, -ae, f. = rod
percutiō, -ere, percussī = I
strike
sus, suis, c. = pig
vertō, -ere, vertī = I turn
relīquus, -a, -um = remaining
fābula, -ae, f. = story

1 Ulixēs cum comitibus ōlim ad īnsulam Aeaeam nāvigāvit (line 1). Where and with whom was Ulysses travelling?

2 in īnsulā habitābat Circe, dea propter artem magicam nōta (lines 1–2). Who or what was Circe?

3 Ulixēs, ubi ad īnsulam advēnit, prope mare, prope nāvem manēbat (lines 2–3). What did Ulysses do when he arrived at the island?

4 aliōs comitēs manēre, aliōs cum Eurylochō ... aquam petere iussit (lines 3–4). How did Ulysses organise his men when they arrived on the island?

5 cum Eurylochō, virō validō et nōtō (line 4). How is Eurylochus described?

6 'festīnāte!' inquit Ulixes. 'aquam et cibum invenīte et ad nāvem portāte!' (lines 5–6). What did Ulysses order his men to do?

7 Eurylochus et comitēs in partem interiōrem īnsulae festīnāvērunt (line 7). Where did Eurylochus and his companions make for?

8 magnam domum in mediā silvā vīdērunt (line 8). What did they see when they got there?

9 prope domum multa animālia errābant (lines 8–9). Who or what did they see near the building?

10 tum dea pulchra ad Graecōs appropinquāvit et cibum dedit (line 9). What happened next?

11 laetī erant et deam laudāvērunt (lines 9–10). What was the reaction of the Greeks?

12 Eurylochus sōlus deam timēbat nec in domum deae intrāvit (lines 10–11). How was Eurylochus's reaction different from that of his companions?

13 subitō dea saeva virōs virgā percussit et in suēs vertit (line 11). What did Circe do suddenly?

14 Eurylochus ... inquit (lines 12–15). Translate these lines.

Go further

In the middle

There are some adjectives in Latin which we use as nouns in English.

A good example of this is medius = middle. Where we in English say 'the middle of the island', in Latin they appear to have said 'the middle island'. A similar thing happens with summus = top.

E.g. in mediam īnsulam = into the middle *of* the island

E.g. ad summum montem = to the top *of* the mountain

◯ Future tense of sum

The future tense of sum has endings which rhyme with the future endings of amō and moneō, and are therefore quite easy to recognise.

1st person singular	erō	I shall be
2nd person singular	eris	You will be
3rd person singular	erit	He/she/it will be
1st person plural	erimus	We shall be
2nd person plural	eritis	You will be
3rd person plural	erunt	They will be

Exercise 2.7

Translate into English:

1 mīles Rōmānus semper erō.

2 tū rēx numquam eris.

3 puella pulchra uxor rēgis erit.

4 iuvenis cārus rēgīnae erit.

5 sociī Graecōrum erimus.

6 vōs tūtī semper eritis.

7 meī comitēs perterritī erunt.

8 mox dux fessus erit.

9 hostēs diū saevī erunt.

10 senex laetus semper erō.

Exercise 2.8

Study the following passage and answer the questions below.

Ulysses to the rescue

Ulixēs, ubi Eurylochus dē comitibus nārrāvit, per <u>silvās</u> ad <u>domum</u> deae
festīnābat. in itinere nūntium deōrum, <u>Mercurium</u>, dux Graecus vīdit.
deus auxilium ducī dare cupiēbat. 'frūstrā contrā deam pugnābis' inquit.
'meō tamen auxiliō tūtus eris.' tum <u>herbam</u> <u>magicam</u> dedit et multa* dē
5 deā monēbat.
  Ulixēs ad <u>domum</u> deae appropinquāvit. multa <u>animālia</u> vīdit et clāmōrēs
audīvit. comitēs tamen nōn vīdit. subitō dea Circe advēnit et ducem
<u>virgā</u> <u>percussit</u>. 'comitēs tuōs' inquit 'in <u>suēs</u> <u>vertī</u> et nunc tū quoque <u>sus</u>
eris!' Ulixēs tamen, auxiliō deī, tūtus erat. Circe īrāta clāmāvit sed
10 tandem Graecōs īn <u>formam</u> <u>hūmānam</u> <u>reddidit</u>.

*See multa = many things, below

silva, -ae, f. = wood	percutiō, -ere, percussī = I strike
domum (acc. f.) = house	sus, suis, c. = pig
Mercurius, -ī, m. = Mercury	vertō, -ere, vertī = I turn
herba, -ae, f. = herb	forma, -ae, f. = form
magicus, -a, -um = magic	hūmānus, -a, -um = human
animal, animalis, n. = animal	reddō, -ere, reddidī = I return
virga, -ae, f. = rod	

1 Translate the passage into English.

2 From the passage, give an example of each of the following:

  (a) a 3rd declension neuter noun

  (b) a preposition followed by the ablative

  (c) an adverb

  (d) a verb in the future tense

3 dedit (line 4).

  (a) Give the person of this verb.

  (b) Give the tense of this verb.

  (c) Give the first person singular, present tense of this verb.

4 clāmōrēs (line 6).

  (a) In which case is this noun?

  (b) Why is this case used?

5 advēnit (line 7). Explain the connection between this word and the English word advent.

6 festīnābat (line 2). This means **he hurried**. How would you say in Latin **he hurries**?

7 Translate the following sentences into Latin:

(a) The inhabitant was warning the sailor.

(b) We shall carry the big shields.

> ## multa = many things
>
> Where in Latin an adjective is used without a noun, we do something called 'understanding' (that is, translating as if the missing word were there), using the gender of the adjective to guide us.
>
> Thus:
>
> multī (with no noun) = many men
>
> multae (with no noun) = many women
>
> multa (with no noun) = many things

◯ Julius Caesar

Perhaps the most famous Roman of all time, Julius Caesar was born in 100 BC. He was a very successful general, and greatly extended Roman rule, notably through the Gallic Wars during which he conquered most of what we now call France and Germany. During this period, Caesar made two invasions of Britain, in 55 and 54 BC. The first invasion was hampered by poor weather, and after a limited success against the Britons the Romans withdrew back to Gaul to regroup. The following year they returned with five legions and advanced into Britain as far as the River Thames. Once again they were plagued by bad weather, which forced Caesar to return to the shore to repair his ships. The Britons were well led by their leader, Cassivellaunus, but eventually the Romans managed to defeat them before returning to Gaul with hostages and the promise of an annual tribute. It would be another hundred years before the Romans returned.

This topic is part of the Non-Linguistic Studies section of the ISEB syllabus.

Exercise 2.9

Study the following passage and answer the questions below.

Caesar's first invasion of Britain, 55 BC

Caesar, postquam Galliam vīcit, in Britanniam venīre cupiēbat. duās
legiōnēs collēgit, septimam et decimam, et multīs cum nāvibus trāns
mare nāvigāvit. ubi advēnērunt, Rōmānī multōs incolās saevōs et multa
esseda prope ōram vīderunt. ad ancorās manēbant nec tamen in mare,
5 quod altum erat, dēsilīre cupiēbant. tandem mīles quī decimae legiōnis
aquilam portābat 'dēsilīte' inquit 'mīlitēs, nisi cupitis aquilam hostibus
prōdere. ego patriam et ducem meum servābō.' tum mīles in mare
dēsiluit et cum incolīs pugnābat. multī Rōmānī statim in mare altum
dēsiluērunt et mox barbarōs* superāvērunt.
10 post proelium tamen tempestās magna coorta est et nāvēs Rōmānōrum
dēlēvit. Caesar et mīlitēs cibum nōn habēbant et mox in Galliam redīre
cōnstituērunt.

* The Romans referred to those who were not Roman citizens as barbarians.

legiō, -ōnis, f. = legion	aquila, -ae, f. = eagle, standard of
colligō, -ere, collēgī = I gather	legion
essedum, -ī, n. = war-chariot	nisi = unless
ōra, -ae, f. = shore	prōdō, -ere = I betray
ad ancorās maneō = I lie at anchor	barbarī, -ōrum, m. pl. = barbarians
nec tamen = but ... not	tempestās, -ātis, f. = storm
dēsiliō, -īre, dēsiluī = I jump down	coorta est = arose
quī = who	

1 Translate the passage into English.

2 From the passage, give in Latin one example of each of the following:

   (a) a present infinitive

   (b) a verb in the future tense

   (c) an adverb

   (d) an imperative

3 dēlēvit (line 11).

   (a) Give the person of this verb.

   (b) Give the tense of this verb.

   (c) Give the first person singular, present tense of this verb.

4 incolīs (line 8).

   (a) In which case is this noun?

   (b) Why is this case used?

5 servābō (line 7). This means **I shall save**. How would you say in Latin **I was saving**?

6 cōnstituērunt (line 12). Explain the connection between this word and the English word **constitution**.

7 Translate the following sentences into Latin, using the vocabulary given below:

   (a) The messenger was announcing the delay.

   (b) We were giving gifts to the Greeks.

messenger = nūntius, -ī, m.	I give = dō, dare, dedī, datum
I announce = nūntiō (1)*	gift = dōnum, -ī, n.
delay = mora, -ae, f.	Greek = Graecus, -a, -um

* If a verb is entirely regular, it is common practice simply to put its conjugation number in brackets, rather than giving its principal parts.

◯ Vocabulary 2

Latin	English
Nouns	
cīvis, cīvis, c.	citizen
hostis, hostis, c.	enemy
iuvenis, iuvenis, c.	young man, young person
mare, maris, n.	sea
mōns, montis, m.	mountain
nāvis, nāvis, f.	ship
senex, senis, m.	old man
urbs, urbis, f.	city
Adjectives	
cārus, -a, -um	dear
cēterī, -ae, -a	the rest, others
longus, -a, -um	long
medius, -a, -um	middle
Verbs	
appropinquō, -āre, -āvī, -ātum	I approach
errō, -āre, -āvī, -ātum	I wander
exspectō, -āre, -āvī, -ātum	I wait for

Slavery

One of the least attractive aspects of the Roman world was the existence of slavery. In the story of Odysseus and Circe, the enchantress turned men into pigs and kept them in captivity for her own amusement. But it wasn't just in stories: the Romans kept men in captivity as slaves, as the Greeks had before them. Slaves could be bought and sold from dealers called vēnāliciī or mangōnēs and became the property of their owners until such time as the owners decided to give them their freedom. Some lived and worked in households with their owners; others worked on large farms or in the mines. Their treatment varied, but beatings were common and it was not unheard of for a slave to be killed by his master (although this was illegal).

If a slave had been loyal and hard-working, he might be granted his freedom or manumissiō, at which point his status changed from slave to that of freedman or libertus.

> This topic is part of the Non-Linguistic Studies section of the ISEB syllabus.

■ Slaves preparing wine – from a Roman stone relief

Exercise 2.10

(a) (i) Tell the story of what happened when Circe turned Odysseus's men into pigs.

   (ii) Give two reasons why Odysseus's men would have considered him to be an exceptional leader.

(b) (i) Describe what it was like to be a slave in Ancient Rome.

   (ii) Which features of ancient slavery do you consider to have been most unfair?

3 The future tense (contd.); nōnne and num

Future of regō, audiō and capiō

The future tense of verbs of the 3rd, 4th and mixed conjugations is markedly different from that of verbs of the 1st and 2nd. It is very easy to confuse these endings with the present tense endings of moneō, so you need to take great care.

1st person singular	reg-am	audi-am	capi-am
2nd person singular	reg-ēs	audi-ēs	capi-ēs
3rd person singular	reg-et	audi-et	capi-et
1st person plural	reg-ēmus	audi-ēmus	capi-ēmus
2nd person plural	reg-ētis	audi-ētis	capi-ētis
3rd person plural	reg-ent	audi-ent	capi-ent

Exercise 3.1

Translate into English:

1 bibet.

2 regēmus.

3 cōnstituam.

4 currētis.

5 dīcam.

6 discēdent.

7 dūcet.

8 legam.

9 lūdēs.

10 mittent.

11 ostendam.

12 pōnētis.

13 scrībēs.

14 cōnspiciet.

15 accipient.

16 effugiēmus.

17 cupiētis.

18 faciam.

19 iaciet.

20 fugient.

Exercise 3.2

Translate into Latin:

1 He will hear.
2 They will drink.
3 I shall capture.
4 We shall decide.
5 She will run.
6 You (sing.) will depart.
7 We shall sleep.
8 I shall lead.
9 They will make.
10 We shall throw.

11 You (pl.) will read.
12 We shall send.
13 I shall show.
14 We shall place.
15 He will rule.
16 She will write.
17 They will come.
18 I shall receive.
19 We shall flee.
20 They will escape.

Exercise 3.3

Translate into English. Take great care over the tense of the verbs in these sentences.

1 uxor ducis templum dēlet.

2 comitēs iuvenis in agrīs manent.

3 vir lūcem clāram coniugī ostendet.

4 hostēs senēs in mare dūcent.

5 mīlitēs multa vulnera in proeliō accipient.

6 paucās nāvēs ad īnsulam nāvigāre cōnstituistis.

7 corpora multōrum mīlitum mortuōrum cōnspeximus.

8 paucī dōna ā rēge saevō accipient.

9 senex ē proeliō saevō sōlus effūgit.

10 paucī nautae ab īnsulā deae vīvī effūgērunt.

◯ nēmō and nihil

These two nouns are a little peculiar. nēmō = no one is a 3rd declension, common noun which declines as follows:

Nom.	nēmō
Acc.	nēminem
Gen.	nūllius
Dat.	nēminī
Abl.	nūllō

nihil = nothing is a neuter noun which we will only see used in the nominative and accusative. It does have other forms but we don't need to worry about them at this stage.

◯ nōnne and num

We have already learnt how to ask questions in Latin, using either -ne or a questioning word such as quis?, cūr? or ubi?

If, however, we wish to ask a question which expects either a positive or a negative answer, we use nōnne or num: nōnne expects the answer yes, num expects the answer no.

E.g. nōnne mātrem tuam amās? = You love your mother, don't you?

E.g. num aquam timēs? = You are not afraid of the water, are you?

◯ et ... et

The Latin for 'both ... and' is et ... et.

E.g. et puerī et puellae in templum festīnābant = Both the boys and the girls were hurrying into the temple.

Exercise 3.4

Translate into English:

1 cūr in agrīs ambulābās?

2 dormiēsne in urbe magnā?

3 num in agrīs currētis?

4 nōnne cīvis ē nāve discessit?

5 et magister et poēta puerīs legent.

6 ubi labōrābātis, agricolae?

7 quis incolās patriae reget?

8 nōnne magister puerōs et puellās terret?

9 et puerī et puellae vulnera habent.

10 quid rēx virō nōtō dedit?

Exercise 3.5

Translate into Latin:

1 The farmer loves both his wife and his daughter, doesn't he?

2 Will the woman hurry into the city of the enemy?

3 Will the leader wait for the remaining soldiers?

4 The young man has not read the book, has he?

5 We will overcome the enemy soon, won't we?

6 Why are both the tired man and the slave-girl standing near the river?

7 Where will you place the dead leader's body?

8 Will the slaves send the poet to the king?

9 What have the slave-girls prepared for the woman?

10 The enemy will not overcome the Roman citizens, will they?

Exercise 3.6

Study the following passage and answer the questions below.

Caesar's second invasion of Britain, 54 BC

Caesar, quod <u>barbarōs</u> superāre cupiēbat, quīnque <u>legiōnēs</u> trāns mare in
Britanniam dūxit. mīlitēs, ubi advēnērunt, <u>ancorās iēcērunt</u> et in mare
<u>dēsiluērunt</u>. ad flūmen Rōmānī iter fēcērunt et hostēs cum <u>equitibus</u> et
<u>essedīs</u> cōnspexērunt. diū <u>pugnātum est</u> sed tandem mīlitēs <u>legiōnis</u>
5 septimae <u>testūdinem</u> fēcērunt et ad <u>mūnitiōnēs</u> hostium <u>aggerem</u>
<u>adiēcērunt</u>. tum locum cēpērunt et hostēs ē <u>silvīs</u> expulērunt.
    postrīdiē <u>tempestās</u> magna <u>coorta est</u> et multās nāvēs Rōmānōrum
dēlēvit. Caesar mīlitēs ad <u>lītus</u> dūxit et nāvēs <u>refēcit</u>. tum iterum ad
<u>castra</u> hostium cōpiās redūxit. hīc <u>barbarōs</u> invēnit cum duce, nōmine
10 Cassivellaunō. <u>hic</u> dux clārus erat et prope flūmen <u>Tamesim</u> Rōmānōs
exspectābat. Caesar cōpiās hostium in <u>rīpā</u> flūminis cōnspexit et mīlitēs
suōs oppugnāre iussit. in flūmen ruērunt ubi multās <u>sudēs acūtās</u>, et in
<u>rīpā</u> et sub aquā, invēnērunt. tandem Rōmānī hostēs superāvērunt et mox
Cassivellaunus <u>pācem petīvit</u>. tum Caesar cum cōpiīs et multīs <u>obsidibus</u>
15 in Galliam revēnit.

barbarī, -ōrum, m. pl. = barbarians	coorta est = arose
legiō, -ōnis, f. = legion	lītus, lītoris, n. = shore
ancorās iaciō = I cast anchor	reficiō, -ere, refēcī = I repair
dēsiliō, -īre, dēsiluī = I jump down	castra, -ōrum, n. pl. = camp
equitēs, equitum, m. pl. (3) = cavalry	hic = this man, he (emphatic)
essedum, -ī, n. = war-chariot	Tamesis (acc. Tamesim) = Thames
pugnātum est = the battle raged	rīpa, -ae, f. = river bank
testūdō, -inis, f. = a tortoise formation	sudis, -is, f. = stake
mūnitiō, -ōnis, f. = a fortification	acūtus, -a, -um = sharp
aggerem adiciō = I throw up a rampart	pāx, pācis, f. = peace
silva, -ae, f. = wood	petō, -ere, petīvī = I seek
postrīdiē = on the next day	obses, obsidis, c. = hostage
tempestās, -ātis, f. = storm	

1 Caesar ... in Britanniam dūxit (lines 1–2).

   (a) Why did Caesar sail to Britain?

   (b) Who or what did he take with him?

2 mīlitēs, ubi advēnērunt, ancorās iēcērunt et in mare dēsiluērunt (lines 2–3).
   What two things are we told about the soldiers on their arrival in Britain?

3 ad flūmen Rōmānī iter fēcērunt et hostēs cum equitibus et essedīs
   cōnspexērunt (lines 3–4). What did the Romans see at the end of their journey?

4 diū pugnātum ... aggerem adiēcērunt (lines 4–6).

    (a) Give two military tactics that the Romans employed during the battle.

    (b) Which of the legions was involved in this?

5 tum locum cēpērunt et hostēs ē silvīs expulērunt (line 6). What was the result of these tactics?

6 nāvēs (line 7).

    (a) Give the case of this noun.

    (b) Why is it in this case?

7 dēlēvit (line 8).

    (a) In which tense is this verb?

    (b) Give the 1st person singular of the present tense.

8 iterum (line 8). What type of word is this?

9 hostium (line 9).

    (a) Give the case and number of this noun.

    (b) Give its nominative singular.

10 clārus (line 10). Explain the connection between this word and the English word **clarity**.

11 exspectābat (line 11). This means **he waited**. How would you say in Latin **he will wait**?

12 rīpā (line 11).

    (a) In which case is this noun?

    (b) Why is this case used?

13 cōnspexit (line 11).

    (a) In which tense is this verb?

    (b) Give its 1st person singular, present tense.

    (c) Give its present infinitive.

14 From lines 7–15 (postrīdie ... revēnit), give one example of each of the following:

    (a) a neuter 3rd declension noun

    (b) a preposition followed by the ablative

    (c) a preposition followed by the accusative

    (d) an adjective

    (e) a present infinitive

15 Translate lines 7–15 of the passage (postrīdie ... revēnit) into English.

The Roman army

Caesar's soldiers would have been much better equipped than the British tribesmen led by Cassivellaunus. Each legion, led by a legatus, would have numbered around 5,300 men. This was divided into ten cohorts, each made up of six centuries.

Soldiers carried a gladius (sword), a pīlum (spear), a pugiō (dagger) and a scūtum (shield). They wore a galea (helmet), lōrica (breastplate) and caligae (sandals).

They would have used catapults such as the tormentum, the onager and the ballista. When attacking enemy fortifications, they would often form a testūdō (tortoise) by holding up their shields to form a covering for their heads and sides.

> This topic is part of the Non-Linguistic Studies section of the ISEB syllabus.

■ A Roman soldier

Revision of verbs. Which part of which verb are the following? Translate them into English.

1	abest	11	habent
2	accipiēs	12	iaciunt
3	aderant	13	iube
4	appropinquābitis	14	lūdere
5	audient	15	mittēmus
6	bibēbat	16	ostendunt
7	cōnspexit	17	rīdētis
8	dēlēte	18	stetit
9	errant	19	erat
10	fugient	20	esse

Exercise 3.8

Revision of nouns. Which part of which noun are the following? Where necessary, other Latin words are included to make clear which case is being used. Translate them into English.

1	aquam	11	cum parentibus
2	cīvium	12	pecūnia
3	ad comitēs	13	ō poēta
4	coniugī	14	rēgīna
5	cum fīliā	15	rēgī
6	in flūmina	16	senis
7	mīles	17	urbs
8	dē montibus	18	cum uxōre
9	in nāvēs	19	virtūtis
10	nōminum	20	in vulnera

Exercise 3.9

Study the following passage and answer the questions below.

Circe warns Ulysses of the dangers that lie ahead

Ulixēs, quod ad patriam suam <u>revenīre</u> cupiēbat, ab īnsulā deae <u>Circēs</u>
discēdere parābat. dea autem <u>eum</u> amābat et dē multīs perīculīs monuit.
'prope īnsulam nāvigābis ubi habitant <u>Sirēnēs</u>,' inquit. 'vōcēs pulchrās
habent sed saevae sunt et tē occīdere cupient. posteā cavē <u>Scyllam</u> et
5 <u>Charybdem</u>! <u>dēnique</u> ad īnsulam <u>Sōlis</u> appropinquābis. <u>sī</u> <u>bovēs</u> <u>Sōlis</u>
cōnsūmēs, numquam <u>domum</u> vidēbis.' Ulixēs, ubi ā <u>Circe</u> discessit,
vōcēs <u>Sirēnum</u> audīre cupiēbat. nautās igitur <u>cēram</u> in <u>aurēs</u> pōnere iussit
et 'mē <u>mālō</u> <u>vincīte</u>!' inquit. ubi autem ad īnsulam appropinquābat,
Ulixēs nautīs clāmāvit. 'festīnāte ad īnsulam' inquit, 'comitēs meī. ad
10 vōcēs pulchrās festīnāte!' vōcem tamen ducis nautae nōn audiēbant et ad
<u>salūtem</u> nāvigāvērunt.
tum Ulixēs et comitēs prope duo <u>saxa</u> nāvigābant ubi habitābant <u>Scylla</u> et <u>Charybdis</u>,
<u>mōnstra</u> saeva. <u>Scylla</u> multa <u>capita</u>, multōs <u>pedēs</u> habēbat, et virōs cōnsūmēbat. Charybdis
in marī altō nāvēs <u>ēvertēbat</u>. prope <u>saxum</u> <u>Scyllae</u>
15 Ulixēs nāvem nāvigāre cōnstituit. subitō mōnstrum sex
nautās superāvit et cōnsūmpsit. cēterī Graecī tamen
<u>Charybdem</u> <u>vītāvērunt</u> et ē perīculō discessērunt.

revenio, -īre = I return, come back
Circe, Circēs, f. = Circe
eum = him
Sirēnēs, -um, f. pl. = the Sirens
Scylla, -ae, f. = Scylla
Charybdis, -is, f. = Charybdis
dēnique = finally
Sōl, Sōlis, m. = the sun
sī = if
bōs, bovis, c. = cow
domum (acc.) = home
cēra, -ae, f. = wax
auris, -is, f. = ear
mālus, -ī, m. = mast
vinciō, -īre = I tie, bind
salūs, salūtis, f. = safety
saxum, -ī, n. = rock
mōnstrum, -ī, n. = monster
caput, capitis, n. = head
pēs, pedis, m. = foot
ēvertō, -ere, ēvertī = I overturn

■ The monster Scylla attacks Ulysses and his men – an artist's impression

1 Ulixēs ... discēdere parābat (lines 1–2). Why was Ulysses preparing to leave Circe's island?

2 dea autem eum amābat et dē multīs perīculīs monuit (line 2). Why did Circe warn Ulysses?

3 'vōcēs pulchrās habent sed saevae sunt et tē occīdere cupient...' (lines 3–4). What do we learn about the Sirens in these lines?

4 sī bōvēs Sōlis cōnsūmēs, numquam domum vidēbis (lines 5–6). What was the likely consequence of eating the cattle of the sun?

5 nautās igitur cēram in aurēs pōnere iussit et 'mē mālō vincīte!' inquit (lines 7–8). Why do you think Ulysses gave these instructions to his men?

6 vōcem tamen ducis nautae nōn audiēbant (line 10). Why did Ulysses's men not obey his commands?

7 comitēs (line 12). In which case is this noun?

8 multa (line 13).

   (a) Give the gender of this adjective.

   (b) With which noun does it agree?

9 habēbat (line 13). Give the Latin subject of this verb.

10 cōnsūmēbat (line 14). Give the Latin object of this verb.

11 nāvigāre (line 15). Which part of which verb is this?

12 cōnsūmpsit (line 16). Explain the connection between this word and the English word **consumption**.

13 discessērunt (line 17).

   (a) In which tense is this verb?

   (b) Give its present infinitive.

   (c) How would you say in Latin **they will depart**?

14 From lines 12–17, give an example of each of the following:

   (a) a 3rd declension neuter noun

   (b) a verb in the imperfect tense

   (c) a 2nd declension masculine noun

15 tum ... discessērunt (lines 12–17). Translate these lines into English.

Vocabulary 3

Latin	English
Verbs	
accipiō, -ere, accēpī, acceptum	I receive
cōnspiciō, -ere, cōnspexī, cōnspectum	I catch sight of
effugiō, -ere, effūgī	I escape
fugiō, -ere, fūgī, fugitum	I flee
Adjectives	
mortuus, -a, -um	dead
paucī, -ae, -a	few
sōlus, -a, -um	alone
vīvus, -a, -um	alive
Adverbs	
nōnne?	introduces a question expecting the answer 'yes'
num?	introduces a question expecting the answer 'no'
Nouns	
nēmō, nullius, c.	no one
nihil	nothing
virtus, virtūtis, f.	courage
vōx, vōcis, f.	voice
vulnus, vulneris, n.	wound

Exercise 3.10

(a) (i) Tell the story of Julius Caesar's invasions of Britain in 55 and 54 BC.

   (ii) To what extent were the Britons able to resist the superior military might of the Romans?

(b) (i) Describe (with the aid of diagrams if you wish) the equipment used by Roman soldiers.

   (ii) Give two reasons why you think the Roman army was able to acquire such a large empire.

(c) (i) Describe how Odysseus avoided the dangers of the Sirens.

   (ii) Mention two other dangers that Odysseus was warned he would face before he could reach his home.

The pluperfect tense; numerals 11–20; personal pronouns

◯ The pluperfect tense

The pluperfect tense is used to describe what *had* happened in the past. The endings shown below are added to the perfect stem, and are the same for all conjugations.

1st person singular	amāv-eram	I had loved
2nd person singular	amāv-erās	You had loved
3rd person singular	amāv-erat	He/she/it had loved
1st person plural	amāv-erāmus	We had loved
2nd person plural	amāv-erātis	You had loved
3rd person plural	amāv-erant	They had loved

These endings should be very familiar, as they are simply the imperfect of sum.

Exercise 4.1

Translate into English:

1 nāvigāverāmus.

2 audīverant.

3 vocāverat.

4 biberant.

5 cōnspexeram.

6 cupīverātis.

7 advēnerat.

8 nōn discesserāmus.

9 nōn effūgeram.

10 iusserāmus.

11 dederat.

12 habitāverātis.

13 iēcerat.

14 mīserāmus.

15 occīderam.

16 posuerat.

17 rēxerāmus.

18 aedificāverant.

19 vīderātis.

20 vīceram.

Exercise 4.2

Translate into Latin:

1 I had sailed.

2 You (sing.) had called.

3 You (sing.) had captured.

4 They had departed.

5 She had slept.

6 I had seen.

7 We had not thrown.

8 He had fled.

9 You (pl.) had carried.

10 They had found.

11 He had given.

12 They had read.

13 You (pl.) had stood.

14 We had remained.

15 You (sing.) had lived.

16 I had ruled.

17 She had written.

18 They had feared.

19 We had given.

20 I had come.

Exercise 4.3

Translate into English:

1 mīlitēs oppidum mox cēperant.

2 puellae multōs puerōs vulnerāverant.

3 dux servōs fessōs monuerat.

4 nautae īnsulam vīderant.

5 vōcem puerī fēmina nōn audīverat.

6 dominus saevus amīcum occīderat.

7 incolae iter longum fēcerant.

8 nūntiī flūmen altum vīderant.

9 vōcem ancillae nōn audīveram.

10 iuvenis senem numquam amāverat.

Exercise 4.4

You have now learnt four tenses, plus the present infinitive and imperatives, of all the regular conjugations and sum plus its compounds. Taking care over which endings are being used, translate the following into English:

1 laudāvimus.

2 adesse.

3 terruerat.

4 vēnērunt.

5 pūnīvistis.

6 mānserant.

7 lūdere.

8 nōn aderam.

9 stat.

10 rīsit.

11 cucurrit.

12 amābimus.

13 vincere.

14 festīnāvērunt.

15 erāmus.

16 advēnistī.

17 dūxerat.

18 effugere.

19 occīdite.

20 scrībam.

Exercise 4.5

Translate into Latin:

1 We shall build.

2 To hold.

3 You (sing.) had hurried.

4 We were laughing.

5 They were reading.

6 You (pl.) lead.

7 To be.

8 You (sing.) had escaped.

9 I was not making.

10 She will not work.

11 He had given.

12 I have heard.

13 She was sending.

14 You (pl.) will punish.

15 We were conquering.

16 She has found.

17 To hand over.

18 They had not asked.

19 He has decided.

20 They had not stood.

◯ Numerals 11–20

The cardinals 11–20 are quite easy to recognise, but great care needs to be taken with the spelling. The numbers 18 and 19 translate literally as 'two-from-twenty' and 'one-from-twenty'.

11	XI	ūndecim
12	XII	duodecim
13	XIII	tredecim
14	XIV	quattuordecim
15	XV	quīndecim
16	XVI	sēdecim
17	XVII	septendecim
18	XVIII	duodēvīgintī
19	XIX	ūndēvīgintī
20	XX	vīgintī

Personal pronouns

So far you have met personal pronouns only in the nominative and accusative. We now need to see how they behave in the other cases.

	1st person		2nd person	
Nom.	egŏ	I	tū	You (sing.)
Voc.	–	–	tū	(O) you!
Acc.	mē	me	tē	you
Gen.	meī	of me	tuī	of you
Dat.	mihi	to, for me	tibi	to, for you
Abl.	mē	with, by, from me	tē	with, by, from you
Nom.	nōs	we	vōs	you (pl.)
Voc.	–	–	vōs	(O) you!
Acc.	nōs	us	vōs	you
Gen.	nostrum	of us	vestrum	of you
Dat.	nōbīs	to, for us	vōbīs	to, for you
Abl.	nōbīs	with, by, from us	vōbīs	with, by, from us

Problems can arise with the words nōs and vōs unless you are careful.

1 If the verb is 1st person plural, nōs = 'we' and is used for emphasis. If the verb is anything other than 1st person plural, nōs must mean 'us'.

  E.g. nōs spectāmus = *we* are watching; but

  nōs spectant = they are watching *us*.

2 The same applies for vōs. If the verb is 2nd person plural, vōs = 'you' (nominative or, possibly, vocative) and is used for emphasis. If it is anything else, vōs must be accusative.

  E.g. vōs spectātis = *you* are watching; but

  vōs spectant = they are watching *you*.

3 When using the preposition cum = 'with', it is *joined on* to the ablative of the personal pronouns as follows: mēcum = with me, tēcum = with you, nōbīscum = with us, vōbīscum = with you (pl.).

Go further

The genitive of personal pronouns is not often found, because instead of 'of me' we usually say 'my', instead of 'of you' we say 'your', etc. But the genitive forms do occur, and to complicate things, there are two different forms for 'of us' and 'of you (pl.)' which need to be distinguished. The forms nostrum and vestrum (above) are said to be **partitive genitives**, because they are used after words which express a part (e.g. ūnus nostrum = one of us). But there are also the forms nostrī and vestrī which are **objective genitives**, used after nouns and adjectives in which a verbal notion is prominent (e.g. love of us = amor nostrī).

Exercise 4.6

Study the information above about personal pronouns. Then translate into Latin:

1 To you (sing.)

2 To me

3 We see you (sing.).

4 You (pl.) had seen us.

5 He was watching you (pl.).

6 *You* (sing.) sleep but *we* work.

7 I had given the book to you (sing.).

8 He is walking with me.

9 They will warn us.

10 I will praise you (sing.).

Exercise 4.7

Study the following passage and answer the questions below.

Julius Caesar's encounter with some pirates

Iulius <u>Caesar</u> dux Rōmānus clārus erat. ōlim prope īnsulam Siciliam in nāve parvā cum paucīs amīcīs nāvigābat. <u>pīrātae</u> malī prope nāvem <u>Caesaris</u> forte nāvigābant. ubi <u>Caesarem</u> cōnspexērunt, nāvem ducis clārī oppugnāvērunt. <u>Caesarem</u> cēpērunt et ad īnsulam Siciliam
5 portāvērunt. ibi ducem Rōmānum diū tenēbant.

mox <u>avāritia</u> piratās superāvit. <u>prīnceps</u> comitibus suīs nūntiāvit: 'sī <u>Caesarem</u> hīc tenēbimus, nōnne Rōmānī pecūniam prō amicō nōbīs trādent?' <u>Caesar</u>, ubi <u>hoc</u> audīvit, nōn timēbat. <u>pīrātīs</u> respondit: '<u>asinī</u> estis,' inquit. 'sī pecūniam accipiētis et mē līberābitis, tum ego vōs
10 necābō.' <u>pīrātae</u> rīsērunt. <u>Caesarem</u> līberāvērunt et multam pecūniam ā Rōmānīs accēpērunt. laetī iam erant. nōn autem laetī erant ubi <u>Caesar</u> et multī mīlitēs Rōmānī ad īnsulam Siciliam nāvigāvērunt: Rōmānī saevī <u>pīrātās</u> petīvērunt et occīdērunt.

Adapted from CE 13+ Level 2, January 2013

> Caesar, Caesaris, m. = Caesar
> pirata, -ae, m. = pirate
> avāritia, -ae, f. = greed
> prīnceps, prīncipis, m. = chief, leader
> hoc (acc.) = this
> asinus, -ī, m. = fool

1 Translate the passage into English.

2 nōbīs (line 7).

  (a) In which case is this word?

  (b) Give its nominative form.

3 mē (line 9).

  (a) In which case is this word?   (b) Give its nominative singular.

4 vōs (line 9).

  (a) In which case is this word?   (b) Give its nominative form.

5 What does this story tell us about Julius Caesar? Give reasons for your answer.

Exercise 4.8

Translate into English:

1 multī cīvēs mē audiēbant.

2 mīles saevus nōs spectābit.

3 tē occīdēre semper cupiēbam.

4 nōs mare amāmus, tū timēs.

5 mīlitēs validī vōs capient.

6 Rōmulus, ō Rōmānī, in caelum iter fēcit!

7 Lars Porsenna multōs Rōmānōs cēperat.

8 nunc māter mea tēcum ambulat.

9 nōs legimus, tū dormīs.

10 nōs multa dōna tibi dedimus.

Study the following passage and answer the questions below.

Ulysses and the cattle of the Sun

ubi Ulixēs ē perīculīs Scyllae et Charybdis effūgit, ad īnsulam
Thrināciam nāvigāvit. hīc deus Hyperīōn septem gregēs bovum et
septem gregēs ovium habēbat et amābat. Ulixēs gregēs audiēbat sed,
quod dea dē īnsulā eum monuerat, verba Circēs in mentem vēnērunt.
5 comitēs igitur procul ā terrā nāvigāre iussit.
    Eurylochus autem īrātus erat et 'dūrus es' inquit 'Ulixēs. comitēs tuī
fessī sunt et dormīre cupiunt; edere cupiunt; perīcula maris noctū
timent.'
    Ulixēs virōs audiēbat et tandem ad īnsulam nāvigāre et ad ancorās
10 manēre cōnstituit. comitēs tamen dē perīculīs iterum monuit et bovēs et
ovēs cōnsūmere vetuit. ubi Graecī cibum cōnsūmpsērunt et dormiēbant,
magna tempestās orta est. Ulixēs et comitēs nāvem ē marī trāxērunt et
multōs diēs* dum tempestās saeviēbat prope ōram manēbant. sōlum
cibum suum edēbant nec gregibus Hyperīōnis nocēbant. tandem ubi
15 Ulixēs aberat Eurylochus et Graecī ēsuriēbant et bovēs deī cōnsūmere
cōnstituērunt. pecudēs miserās occīdērunt et deīs sacrificāvērunt. tum
carnem bovum cōnsūmpsērunt.
    Ulixēs īrātus erat sed post septem noctēs tempestās minuēbat et Graecī
ab īnsulā discessērunt. Iuppiter tamen ventum magnum in nāvem iēcit et
20 dēlēvit. Ulixēs sōlus carīnam tenēbat sed cēterī nautae periērunt. tandem
ad īnsulam Ogygiam, domum deae Calypsūs, Ulixēs advēnit.

*A period of time is expressed in Latin by the accusative case: 'for many days'

Scylla, -ae, f. = Scylla	multōs diēs = for many days
Charybdis, -is, f. = Charybdis	dum = while
Thrinācia, -ae, f. = Thrinacia	saeviō, -īre = I rage
grex, gregis, m. = flock, herd	ōra, -ae, f. = shore
bōs, bovis, c. = cow (pl. = cattle)	Hyperīōn, -ōnis, m. = Hyperion (the sun god)
ovis, ovis, f. = sheep	noceō, -ēre (+ dat.) = I harm
Circēs (gen.) = of Circe (a goddess)	ēsuriō, -īre = I am hungry
mēns, mentis, f. = mind	pecus, pecudis, f. = beast
procul = far	carō, carnis, f. = flesh
edō, edere, ēdī = I eat	nox, noctis, f. = night
noctū = at night	minuō, -ere = I die down, lessen
ad ancorās maneō = I wait at anchor	carīna, -ae, f. = keel
vetō, -āre, vetuī = I forbid	Ogygia, -ae, f. = Ogygia (an island)
tempestās, -ātis, f. = storm	domum (acc.) = home
orta est = (it) arose	Calypsūs (gen.) = of Calypso (a goddess)
trahō, -ere, trāxī = I drag	

1 ubi … nāvigāvit (lines 1–2). What did Ulysses do after escaping from Scylla and Charybdis?

2 hīc deus Hyperīōn septem gregēs bovum et septem gregēs ovium habēbat et amābat (lines 2–3). What do we learn about the god Hyperion in these lines?

3 Ulixēs … vēnerunt (lines 3–4). What happened when Ulysses heard the cattle lowing, and why?

4 comitēs … iussit (line 5). What instruction did Ulysses give as a result?

5 Eurylochus … Ulixēs (line 6). How did Eurylochus respond to Ulysses's command?

6 comitēs … timent (lines 6–8). Which three reasons did he give for challenging Ulysses's command?

7 Ulixēs virōs … cōnstituit (lines 9–10). What was the effect on Ulysses of Eurylochus's speech?

8 comitēs tamen … vetuit (lines 10–11).

   (a) What warning did Ulysses give?

   (b) Give and translate the Latin word which tells us that this warning had been given before.

9 Ulixēs et comitēs … manēbant (lines 12–13). What did the Greeks do when the storm blew up?

10 tandem … cōnsūmpsērunt (lines 14–17). What do we learn in these lines about what happened while Ulysses was absent?

11 noctēs (line 18).

   (a) In which case is this noun?

   (b) Why is this case used?

12 discessērunt (line 19).

   (a) In which tense is this verb?

   (b) Give the 1st person singular of the present tense.

13 magnum (line 19).

   (a) In which case is this word?

   (b) With which word does it agree?

14 dēlēvit (line 20). This means **he destroyed**. How would you say in Latin **he will destroy**?

15 sōlus (line 20). Explain the connection between this word and the English word **solo**.

16 nautae (line 20). Explain the connection between this word and the English word **nautical**.

17 advēnit (line 21). Give this verb's present infinitive.

18 Translate lines 6–17 (Eurylochus … cōnsūmpsērunt).

Translate into English:

1 dux ad īnsulam cum vigintī comitibus advēnit.

2 Graecī cibum et aquam in īnsulā invēnērunt.

3 deus mīlitēs pūnīre cōnstituerat.

4 quīndecim iuvenēs dōnum rēgī trādidērunt.

5 Caesar ad īnsulam advēnit et incolās vīcit.

6 nōnne iuvenis cārus ducī erat?

7 clāmōrēs sēdecim mīlitum audīvimus.

8 num trāns ūndecim flūmina iter faciēmus?

9 paucī cīvēs vulnera accēperant.

10 nēmō pecūniam cēterīs mulieribus trādere cupiēbat.

⬡ Vocabulary 4

Latin	English
Verbs	
adveniō, -īre, advēnī, adventum	I arrive
inveniō, -īre, invēnī, inventum	I find
pūniō, -īre, pūnīvī, pūnītum	I punish
trādō, -ere, trādidī, trāditum	I hand over
vincō, -ere, vīcī, victum	I conquer
Numbers	
ūndecim	eleven
duodecim	twelve
tredecim	thirteen
quattuordecim	fourteen
quīndecim	fifteen
sēdecim	sixteen
septendecim	seventeen
duodēvīgintī	eighteen
ūndēvīgintī	nineteen
vīgintī	twenty

The theatre

The Romans loved stories about the heroes of mythology, and a very popular pastime was to go to the theatre, where these stories might be acted out. A typical Roman theatre was open-air and built around a semicircular stage. At the back of the stage was a permanent structure called the scaena, often painted to look like a house, and in front of the stage the most important people sat on chairs in an area called the orchestra. Tiers of seats rose up above the orchestra, with the least important spectators sitting furthest from the stage. If it was very hot, the theatre could be covered by awnings called vēlāria.

The actors wore masks and wigs and these were often coloured to show the type of character they represented: brown masks for males, white for female, white wigs for old men, red for slaves.

This topic is part of the Non-Linguistic Studies section of the ISEB syllabus.

■ The Roman theatre at Bosra in Syria

Exercise 4.11

(a) (i) Tell the story of Odysseus and the cattle of the sun.

(ii) Why do you think Odysseus's men disobeyed his warnings about the cattle?

(b) (i) Give an account of a visit to the theatre in Roman times.

(ii) In what ways would a visit to a Roman theatre have differed from a visit to a modern theatre?

5 3rd declension adjectives; is, ea, id

3rd declension adjectives

All the adjectives you have met so far have been 1st or 2nd declension (like bonus, miser or pulcher). These adjectives, as you know, take their endings from the 1st and 2nd declensions. But a large number of adjectives take their endings from the 3rd declension.

One termination adjectives

Some 3rd declension adjectives decline like ingēns:

ingēns, ingentis = huge			
	Masculine	Feminine	Neuter
Nom.	ingēns	ingēns	ingēns
Voc.	ingēns	ingēns	ingēns
Acc.	ingent-em	ingent-em	ingēns
Gen.	ingent-is	ingent-is	ingent-is
Dat.	ingent-ī	ingent-ī	ingent-ī
Abl.	ingent-ī	ingent-ī	ingent-ī
Nom.	ingent-ēs	ingent-ēs	ingent-ia
Voc.	ingent-ēs	ingent-ēs	ingent-ia
Acc.	ingent-ēs	ingent-ēs	ingent-ia
Gen.	ingent-ium	ingent-ium	ingent-ium
Dat.	ingent-ibus	ingent-ibus	ingent-ibus
Abl.	ingent-ibus	ingent-ibus	ingent-ibus

Other adjectives that go like ingēns are:
audāx, audācis = bold
fēlīx, fēlīcis = fortunate, happy
sapiēns, sapientis = wise

Adjectives like ingēns have endings taken from the 3rd declension, but the following points should be noted:

1 The endings for the nominative singular are the same for all three genders, and thus ingēns is said to be a **one termination** adjective.

2 One termination adjectives are always listed in the vocabulary with their nominative and genitive singular (e.g. ingēns, ingentis). By taking the genitive singular and chopping off the -is, we are left with the stem. It is to this that the endings are added.

3 The ablative singular ends in -ī, not -e.

4 In the plural, ingēns behaves like a non-increasing noun, adding an i to the genitive plural (-ium) and to the first three cases in the neuter (-ia).

Exercise 5.1

Study the information above about 3rd declension adjectives. Notice how one termination adjectives are always listed in the vocabulary with their nominative and genitive singular forms. Then translate into English:

1 īnsulam ingentem mox vīdimus.

2 mīlitem audācem gladiō ingentī necāvit.

3 agricola sub mūrō ingentī dormiēbat.

4 scūta ingentia in puellam miseram iēcērunt.

5 cīvēs audācēs flūmen ingēns nōn timuērunt.

6 Ulixēs cum comite audācī ambulābat.

7 incolae fēlīcēs ab oppidō effūgērunt.

8 rēx saevus poētam sapientem invēnit.

9 rēgīna ancillās sapientēs nōn amābat.

10 incolae Rōmānī templa ingentia semper aedificābant.

Adjectival agreement

Take care when making 3rd declension adjectives agree with nouns. Exactly the same rules apply as for all types of adjective agreement. The noun is written first; then you work out which case, gender and number the noun is; then you put the adjective into that form.

E.g. Of the farmer:
Masculine, genitive singular
= agricolae

Of the *huge* farmer
= agricolae ingentis

Exercise 5.2

Translate into Latin:

1 Of the fortunate farmer
2 Of the huge rivers
3 The bold girl (nom.)
4 The bold girls (acc.)
5 Towards the huge temple
6 With the bold soldiers
7 Near the fortunate leader
8 The huge swords (nom.)
9 Across the huge wall
10 With the bold sailor

Exercise 5.3

Translate into English:

1 mīlitēs Rōmānī hostēs prope flūmen ingēns oppugnābant.
2 hostēs autem mūrum ingentem prope flūmen parāverant.
3 Lars Porsenna, rēx hostium, mīlitēs audācēs ad Rōmānōs dūxit.
4 Rōmānī autem hostēs audācēs nōn timēbant et in proelium festīnāvērunt.
5 hostēs Rōmānōs audācēs vīdērunt nec tamen* fugere cupiēbant.
6 ego virtūtem mīlitum audācium iam laudāveram.
7 parentēs mihi nōmen poētae fēlīcis dedērunt.
8 amīcus fēlīx mēcum in templum ingēns festīnāverat.
9 iuvenēs audācēs cum servīs fēlīcibus bibēbant.
10 homō fēlīx coniugem semper amābit.

*Remember, the Latin for 'but not' is nec tamen. Do NOT write sed followed by non.

Two termination adjectives

You have now met a 3rd declension adjective and realised how easy it was. But most 3rd declension adjectives are not one termination, like ingēns, but *two termination*, like trīstis:

trīstis, trīste = sad, gloomy			
	Masculine	**Feminine**	**Neuter**
Nom.	trīstis	trīstis	trīst-e
Voc.	trīstis	trīstis	trīst-e
Acc.	trīst-em	trīst-em	trīst-e
Gen.	trīst-is	trīst-is	trīst-is
Dat.	trīst-ī	trīst-ī	trīst-ī
Abl.	trīst-ī	trīst-ī	trīst-ī
Nom.	trīst-ēs	trīst-ēs	trīst-ia
Voc.	trīst-ēs	trīst-ēs	trīst-ia
Acc.	trīst-ēs	trīst-ēs	trīst-ia
Gen.	trīst-ium	trīst-ium	trīst-ium
Dat.	trīst-ibus	trīst-ibus	trīst-ibus
Abl.	trīst-ibus	trīst-ibus	trīst-ibus

1 Trīstis is said to be **two termination** because in the nominative singular it has two different endings, one for the masculine and feminine, and one for the neuter.

2 To show that it is a two termination adjective, the two nominative singular forms are given (trīstis, trīste). This is often abbreviated to trīstis, -e.

3 The stem of two termination adjectives can be found by going to the neuter form (trīste) and chopping off the -e.

Exercise 5.4

Study the information above about 3rd declension adjectives like trīstis. Most 3rd declension adjectives decline like this, so make sure you are thoroughly familiar with it. Write out in full (all three genders, all cases, singular and plural):

1 facilis, facile = easy

2 omnis, omne = all, every

3 crūdēlis, crūdēle = cruel

Exercise 5.5

Translate into Latin:

1 Of the sad king
2 To the sad farmer (dat.)
3 With the sad soldier
4 In the sad books
5 O sad girls!

6 All the books (nom.)
7 Of the cruel leader
8 All the battles (nom.)
9 Of the bold leaders
10 The difficult journey (nom.)

Exercise 5.6

Translate into English:

1 puella dōnum ingēns ad magistrum mīsit.

2 dux fortis multōs mīlitēs in proelium difficile dūcēbat.

3 puerī et puellae dē monte ingentī currēbant.

4 incolae īnsulae trīstēs erant.

5 poēta fēminīs trīstibus iam cantat.

6 dux trīstis cōpiās fortēs in mare dūxerat.

7 nostrī* in marī diū pugnābant et nautās fortēs superābant.

8 māter trīstis fīliam laetam sub mūrō invēnit.

9 cūr aquam ē marī ad urbem portātis?

10 multōs clāmōrēs in montibus audiēbant.

*Remember that adjectives are often used without a noun: nostrī (in the masculine) = 'our men'.

is, ea, id

We already know how to translate 'I' and 'you' and 'we' and 'us'. But what about 'him' and 'her' and 'them'? Here a small problem occurs: there is no 3rd person pronoun in Latin. Instead Latin uses the demonstrative pronoun 'that': it uses it in the masculine to mean 'he', in the feminine to mean 'she' and in the neuter to mean 'it'.

is, ea, id = that (he, she, it)

	M	F	N
Nom.	is	ea	id
Voc.	–	–	–
Acc.	eum	eam	id
Gen.	eius	eius	eius
Dat.	eī	eī	eī
Abl.	eō	eā	eō
Nom.	eī	eae	ea
Voc.	–	–	–
Acc.	eōs	eās	ea
Gen.	eōrum	eārum	eōrum
Dat.	eīs	eīs	eīs
Abl.	eīs	eīs	eīs

1 The forms iī and iīs are sometimes found instead of eī and eīs.

2 Generally, is, ea, id means 'that' or 'those' *when used in agreement with a noun*. When used alone, it means 'he', 'she', 'it' or 'they'.

E.g. agricola eum puerum videt = The farmer sees that boy.

E.g. agricola eum videt = The farmer sees him.

Exercise 5.7

Study the information above about is, ea, id. Then give the Latin for the following. Use pronouns (for emphasis) where italics are used.

1 We love him.

2 You (sing.) hear her.

3 She sees them.

4 We fear it.

5 For him

6 With them

7 Near her

8 *She* is singing.

9 I have found it.

10 *He* loves her.

Exercise 5.8

Translate into Latin:

1 To me
2 From you (sing.)
3 Of him
4 Those soldiers (nom.)
5 For them

6 For you (pl.)
7 With us
8 Me
9 Him
10 For her

Exercise 5.9

Translate into English:

1 dōnum tibi dedī.
2 nōbīs dōna dedit.
3 māter eius
4 id flūmen
5 nōs monētis.

6 cibum eius parābō.
7 ad eum ambulābam.
8 eum librum legit.
9 vōs timētis.
10 nōbīs cantās.

Exercise 5.10

Study the following passage and answer the questions below.

Ulysses, Calypso and the island of the Phaeacians

Ulixēs, ubi ad īnsulam Ogygiam advēnit, deam <u>Calypsō</u> vīdit. ea dea
pulchra erat et statim Ulixem amāvit. per septem <u>annōs</u> dux audāx in
īnsulā cum eā habitābat. tandem ad uxōrem cāram et fīlium <u>revenīre</u>
cōnstituit. auxiliō deae nāvem aedificāvit et ab īnsulā discessit.

5　　Neptūnus deus maris erat. Ulixem deus nōn amābat. ubi nāvem Ulixis in
marī cōnspexit, īrātus erat. 'saevam <u>tempestātem</u>,' inquit, 'in Ulixem
mittam. eum dēlēbō.' Neptūnus <u>tempestātem</u> mīsit et nāvem dēlēvit.
Ulixēs diū in marī <u>natābat</u> et tandem ad <u>lītus</u> īnsulae <u>aliēnae</u> tūtus*
advēnit.

10　　dux audāx sub <u>arbore</u> dormiēbat. ubi <u>sē excitāvit</u>, turbam puellārum
cōnspexit. puellae in flūmine lūdēbant et laetae* rīdēbant. Ulixēs unam
ex eīs, nōmine Nausicaam, salūtāvit. 'quis es?' inquit. 'cupisne mihi
auxilium dare?' puella non timēbat et sīc respondit: 'ego Nausicaa sum,'
inquit. 'māter mea rēgīna est, pater rēx. tē ad urbem dūcam.'

15   Nausicaa cum comitibus Ulixem ad urbem dūxit. celeriter trāns flūmina et per agrōs cucurrērunt, sed prope mūrōs urbis <u>cōnstitērunt</u>. Nausicaa Ulixem iussit ibi manēre, quod cīvēs <u>suspīciōsī</u> erant. Ulixēs ibi <u>breviter</u> manēbat, inde ad <u>vīllam</u> patris puellae festīnāvit.

Adapted from CE 13+ Level 2, November 2013

*Notice how Latin often uses an adjective where we in English would expect an adverb.

Calypsō (acc.) = Calypso, a divine nymph	arbor, arboris, f. = tree
annus, -ī, m. = year	sē excitō, -āre, -āvī = I wake up
reveniō, -īre, revēnī = I return	cōnsistō, -ere, cōnstitī = I stop
tempestās, -ātis, f. = storm	suspīciōsus, -a, -um = suspicious
natō, -āre, -āvī = I swim	breviter = for a short while
lītus, lītoris, n. = shore	vīlla, -ae, f. = house
aliēnus, -a, -um = foreign, unknown	

1 Translate the passage into English.

2 From the passage, give *four* examples of the demonstrative pronoun is, ea, id being used, giving the case, number and gender for each.

3 From the passage, give *three* examples of a personal pronoun being used, for each giving the case and number and saying which pronoun it comes from.

Translating his, her, its and their

1 One way to translate 'his', 'her', 'its' or 'their' is to leave the words out altogether!
   E.g. puer mātrem amat = The boy loves his mother.

2 If, however, we wish to stress or emphasise the fact that by 'his' we mean 'his own', or by 'their' we mean 'their own', etc., we use suus, -a, -um.
   E.g. She sees her (own) brother = suum frātrem videt.
   E.g. They see their (own) mother = suam mātrem vident.

3 Finally, if by 'his' we mean 'someone else's', we use the genitive of is, ea, id.
   E.g. She sees his (i.e. someone else's) friend = eius amīcum videt.
   E.g. She sees their (i.e. not her) mother = eōrum mātrem videt.

Exercise 5.11

Translate into Latin:

1 She loves her mother.

2 They do not love their country.

3 She loves his mother.

4 They love her country.

5 We praise you (sing.) but we do not like him.

6 You (sing.) praise us but you do not like them.

7 They praise those girls but they do not like you (pl.).

8 He loves that girl.

9 He had thrown that spear.

10 The name of that man is well known.

Exercise 5.12

Translate into English:

1 rēx servōs miserōs ad urbem suam mīsit.

2 dominī multōs servōs in templum dūxērunt.

3 fīlia mīlitis eius prope mūrōs ambulābat.

4 hostēs in eam urbem dūcere cupiēbat.

5 hostēs tamen puellam miseram nōn amābant.

6 nōs patriam nostram semper amābimus.

7 in altōs montēs cum amīcīs audācibus iter fēcit.

8 'mē ad id flūmen magnum dūc!' inquit.

9 multa dōna tibi et fīliō tuō iam dedī.

10 quis eōs in mare iacere cupit?

Exercise 5.13

In the early days of the Roman republic there was a constant conflict between the patricians (the aristocratic families descended from the original founders of Rome) and the plebeians (the common citizens). A major grievance of the plebeians was that the laws were not written down, so nobody knew what one was allowed to do. In about 450 BC, ten judges were appointed to study the laws of Athens and then write down a set of laws for Rome. These came to be known as the Twelve Tables.

One of these judges was a man called Appius Claudius. He caused something of
a scandal when he tried to use his power as a judge to get hold of a girl called
Verginia, despite the fact that she was already betrothed to another man. He
persuaded a friend of his, Marcus Claudius, to claim that Verginia was a slave-girl
belonging to him. Marcus brought her to court and the judge in the case was
none other than Appius Claudius. When the girl's father realised that his daughter
was going to be taken from him and given over to the wicked judge, he took
drastic action...

Translate into English:

A Roman father saves his daughter, 449 BC

ōlim cīvis Rōmānus, nōmine Appius Claudius, puellam pulchram,
nōmine Vergīniam, amābat. sed pater Vergīniae eam in <u>mātrimōnium</u>
iam <u>prōmīserat</u>. Appius igitur amīcō suō 'nōnne tū' inquit 'mē
<u>adiuvābis</u>? eam puellam in <u>mātrimōnium dūcere</u> cupiō.' amīcus eius
5   <u>forum</u> intrāvit et Vergīniam cēpit. ea autem fugere cupiēbat sed frūstrā.
pater tamen fīliam vīdit et clāmāvit. 'fīliam meam' inquit 'nōn capiēs.
eam servābō.' inde gladium cēpit et fīliam cāram occīdit. ita puellam
miseram servāvit.

> mātrimōnium, -iī, n. = marriage
> adiuvō, -āre, adiūvī = I help
> prōmittō, -ere, prōmīsī = I promise
> in mātrimōnium dūcō = I marry
> forum, -ī, n. = the forum

1   ōlim cīvis Rōmānus ... amābat (lines 1–2). What do we learn about Appius
    Claudius in these lines?

2   sed pater ... prōmīserat (lines 2–3). What do we learn about Verginia's father
    in these lines?

3   Appius igitur ... dūcere cupiō (lines 3–4). What did Appius say to his friend?

4   amīcus eius forum intrāvit et Vergīniam cēpit (lines 4–5). What did the friend
    do to help?

5   ea autem fugere cupiēbat sed frūstrā (line 5).

    (a) How did Verginia respond?

    (b) Give and translate the Latin word which tells us that this response was
         not successful.

6 pater ... servāvit (lines 6–8). Explain in detail how Verginia's father responded to her plight.

7 eam (line 2).

(a) In which case is this word?

(b) Give its nominative singular (in the same gender).

8 suō (line 3).

(a) In which case is this word?

(b) Give its nominative plural (in the same gender).

9 eius (line 4).

(a) In which case is this word?

(b) Give its nominative singular (in the same gender).

10 ea (line 5).

(a) In which case is this word?

(b) Give its nominative plural (in the same gender).

◯ Vocabulary 5

Latin	English
-que	and
arma, -ōrum, n. pl.	weapons, arms
autem	however, moreover
cōpiae, -ārum, f. pl.	forces
dōnum, -ī, n.	gift
et ... et	both ... and
frāter, frātris, m.	brother
Graecus, -a, -um	Greek
līberī, -ōrum, m. pl.	children
māter, mātris, f.	mother
mōra, -ae, f.	delay
mors, mortis, f.	death
pars, partis, f.	part
pater, patris, m.	father
soror, sorōris, f.	sister

Roman houses

In the story of Verginia, above, when Appius Claudius's friend left to go to the forum, what sort of house do you think he would have left? We know a remarkable amount about Roman housing, not least because the remains of so many were preserved at Pompeii and Herculaneum for almost two thousand years under the volcanic ash of Mount Vesuvius. A typical Roman town house (domus) was built around one or more courtyards. One entered through the ianua (door) into the ātrium (entrance hall). In the roof above the ātrium was an opening, the compluvium, allowing rainwater to fall through into the impluvium, a sunken pool. The master of the house would have welcomed his guests into the ātrium, and here stood the larārium, a shrine containing the household gods. Off the ātrium were reception rooms such as the trīclīnium (dining room) and tablīnum (study), a kitchen (culīna), and bedrooms (cubicula). Passing out through the back of the house one would find a courtyard garden, the peristylium, and perhaps one or more garden rooms such as the oecus (an outdoor dining room) or the exedra (an outdoor sitting room).

> This topic is part of the Non-Linguistic Studies section of the ISEB syllabus.

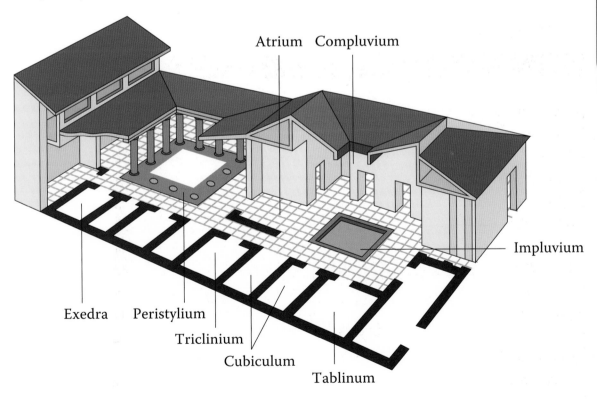

■ A Roman house

(a) (i) Tell the story of Odysseus and Calypso.

   (ii) Who do you think was the greatest help to Odysseus: Calpyso or Circe?

(b) (i) Give an account of a visit to a Roman town house. Draw a diagram to illustrate your account.

   (ii) In what ways would a Roman town house have differed from a modern town house in London?

6 The comparison of adjectives

Regular comparison of adjectives

Adjectives may be compared in three degrees: positive, comparative and superlative. The **positive** is the normal form of the adjective. The **comparative** is formed by adding -ior to the stem of the adjective. The **superlative** is formed by adding -issimus to the stem of the adjective.

Positive	Comparative	Superlative
longus	long-ior	long-issimus
long	longer, more long	longest, most long, very long
trīstis	trīst-ior	trīst-issimus
sad	sadder, more sad	saddest, most sad, very sad

Exercise 6.1

Give the comparative and superlative of:

1 nōtus, -a, -um

2 laetus, -a, -um

3 cārus, -a, -um

4 īrātus, -a, -um

5 altus, -a, -um

6 ingēns, ingentis

7 sapiēns, sapientis

8 fortis, forte

9 fēlīx, fēlīcis

10 audāx, audācis

⬤ Declension of comparative and superlative adjectives

Irrespective of what declension the adjective is to start with, comparatives decline like melior, melius = 'better', and superlatives decline like bonus, -a, -um.

melior, melius = better			
	M	F	N
Nom.	melior	melior	melius
Voc.	melior	melior	melius
Acc.	meliōr-em	meliōr-em	melius
Gen.	meliōr-is	meliōr-is	meliōr-is
Dat.	meliōr-ī	meliōr-ī	meliōr-ī
Abl.	meliōr-e	meliōr-e	meliōr-e
Nom.	meliōr-ēs	meliōr-ēs	meliōr-a
Voc.	meliōr-ēs	meliōr-ēs	meliōr-a
Acc.	meliōr-ēs	meliōr-ēs	meliōr-a
Gen.	meliōr-um	meliōr-um	meliōr-um
Dat.	meliōr-ibus	meliōr-ibus	meliōr-ibus
Abl.	meliōr-ibus	meliōr-ibus	meliōr-ibus

The declension of melior is slightly odd, in that it behaves more like a 3rd declension noun than a 3rd declension adjective. Note its ablative singular form ends in -e (like 3rd declension nouns), and it has no extra i in the plural forms (thus it goes -um rather than -ium in the genitive plural, and -a rather than -ia in the neuter).

Exercise 6.2

Translate into English:

1 mōns altior

2 mīlitēs audāciōrēs

3 rēx crūdēlissimus

4 ō incolae fēlīcissimī!

5 dux fortissimus

6 magister īrātior

7 poēta nōtissimus

8 cum cīve sapientiōre

9 ad virum validissimum

10 bellum saevius

Exercise 6.3

Translate into Latin:

1 Of the sadder girl
2 The braver kings (nom.)
3 The longer wars (nom.)
4 The very angry master (nom.)
5 Of the most happy woman

6 For the most fortunate general
7 With the boldest soldiers
8 On the higher mountain
9 Near the deeper river
10 O most happy farmers!

Comparing nouns

1 Two nouns being compared using quam = 'than' must be in the same case.
   E.g. puella trīstior est quam puer = The girl is sadder than the boy.
2 Alternatively, if two persons or things are **directly compared**, an ablative of comparison may be used, with the second noun being put in the ablative (without quam).
   E.g. puella trīstior est puerō = The girl is sadder than the boy.

Exercise 6.4

Translate into English:

1 mōns altior est quam templum.

2 mare altius est quam omnia flūmina.

3 dux clārior erat quam rēx.

4 nōnne poētam nōtissimum amātis?

5 num mīlitēs saeviōrēs sunt quam agricolae?

6 uxor mea pulchrior est quam ea fēmina.

7 magister īrātior est rēge.

8 nōs tūtiōrēs erāmus quam mīlitēs hostium.

9 trēs comitēs audāciōrēs erant quam dux eōrum.

10 omnēs Rōmānī crūdēliōrēs erant quam Graecī.

Translate into Latin:

1 The king was braver than the queen.

2 The brave Romans fought in a very long war.

3 The Roman soldiers were bolder than the Greeks.

4 Our mother is sadder than your father.

5 Send a nobler leader to the town!

6 Many Romans were overcoming the bolder soldiers.

7 We have a braver leader than you (i.e. than you have).

8 We have a leader, braver than you (i.e. who is braver than you).

9 The mountains are higher than our city.

10 Our leader was stronger than all.

Adjectives in -er and -ilis

Adjectives in -er change -er to -errimus instead of -issimus to form their superlative:

| Beautiful | pulcher | pulchrior | pulcherrimus |

Some adjectives in -ilis go -illimus instead of -issimus:

| Easy | facilis | facilior | facillimus |
| Difficult | difficilis | difficilior | difficillimus |

Irregular comparison

The following common adjectives are irregular in comparison:

Good	bonus	melior	optimus
Bad	malus	peior	pessimus
Big	magnus	maior	maximus
Small	parvus	minor	minimus
Much, many	multus	plūs*	plūrimus

*Plūs, plūris is used in the singular as a neuter noun followed by a genitive.

E.g. He wants more money = plūs pecūniae cupit.

In the plural it is used as an adjective, declining as follows:

	Masc.	Fem.	Neut.
Nom.	plūrēs	plūrēs	plūra
Voc.	plūrēs	plūrēs	plūra
Acc.	plūrēs	plūrēs	plūra
Gen.	plūrium	plūrium	plūrium
Dat.	plūribus	plūribus	plūribus
Abl.	plūribus	plūribus	plūribus

E.g. He wants more forces = plūrēs cōpiās cupit.

Exercise 6.6

Read the information above about adjectives in -er and -ilis and irregular comparison. Give the comparative and superlative of:

1 multus, -a, -um

2 miser, misera, miserum

3 parvus, -a, -um

4 pulcher, pulchra, pulchrum

5 malus, -a, -um

6 magnus, -a, -um

Exercise 6.7

Translate into English:

1 templa nostra maiōra erant quam Graecōrum.

2 puella minor erat quam puer.

3 omnēs incolae erant miserrimī.

4 num omnium fēminārum rēgīna erat pulcherrima?

5 nōnne Tarquinius erat rēx pessimus?

6 equus tuus maior est quam meus.

7 mīlitēs incolās plūrimōs in proeliō occīdērunt.

8 iter difficillimum erat mīlitibus nostrīs.

9 facillimum erat agricolīs equum minimum capere.

10 Ulixēs post bellum longissimum ad īnsulam advēnit.

Exercise 6.8

Give the Latin for:

1. Of the biggest city
2. In the deepest river
3. The most beautiful women (acc.)
4. The worst dangers (nom.)
5. For the bolder soldiers
6. The most difficult war (acc.)
7. On a very easy journey
8. On the easier journeys
9. After the longest war
10. Before the greatest battle

Exercise 6.9

Translate and then give an English word derived from the following, explaining the connection between the English and Latin words.

1. optimus
2. pessimus
3. minimus
4. maximus
5. plūs

Exercise 6.10

Translate into English:

A Pyrrhic victory – the Battle of Heraclea, 280 BC

nunc Rōma erat urbs maxima Ītaliae et multī ā Rōmānīs auxilium petēbant. cīvēs tamen Tarentī Rōmānōs nōn amābant et auxilium ā Graecīs petīvērunt. erat autem in Graeciā rēx nōmine Pyrrhus. is multās terrās regere cupiēbat. postquam* cīvēs Tarentī auxilium petīvērunt,
5 Pyrrhus cum plūrimīs mīlitibus in Ītaliam vēnit. Rōmānōs prope Hēraclēam superāvit, sed Rōmānī plūrimōs mīlitēs Graecōs occīdērunt.
post proelium 'victōriam peperī' inquit rēx 'sed mox nūllōs mīlitēs habebō.'

*See More on conjunctions below

> petō, -ere, petīvī = I seek
> Tarentum, -ī, n. = Tarentum
> victōriam pariō, -ere, peperī = I win a victory
> nūllōs, -a, -um = no, none

More on conjunctions

Postquam is a conjunction and is normally followed by a perfect tense in Latin which is often translated by a pluperfect in English.

E.g. postquam petīvit = after he *had* sought.

Autem means 'however' or 'moreover', but is very often used simply to connect two sentences together, and in such cases need not be translated at all.

E.g. rēx īn forum festīnāvit. cives autem eum timēbant et discessērunt.

The king hurried into the forum. The citizens were afraid of him and left.

More about 'and'

We have already seen that et … et means 'both … and'.

E.g. rēx et agricolās et nautās occīdit.

The king killed both the farmers and the sailors.

But another thing to notice about the word 'and' is that it can be translated by putting -que on the end of a word.

E.g. rēx agricolās nautāsque occīdit.

The king killed the farmers and the sailors.

Exercise 6.11

Study the following passage and answer the questions below.

The homecoming of Ulysses

Nausicaa, postquam Ulixem ad vīllam parentum suōrum dūxit, ducem audācissimum diū audiēbat. is rēgī dē plūrimīs perīculīs itineris nārrāvit auxiliumque <u>petīvit</u>. rēx Ulixem amābat et eī nāvem nautāsque dedit. 'nāvigāte ad īnsulam Ithacam,' inquit, 'et Graecum fortissimum ad
5 uxōrem eius dūcite.'

Ulixēs, ubi in īnsulam advēnit, <u>procōs</u> plūrimōs in <u>vīllā</u> suā invēnit. omnēs uxōrem pulcherrimam Ulixis amābant et eam <u>in mātrimōnium dūcere</u> magnopere cupiēbant. fēminae pulchrae, 'Ulixēs mortuus est,' inquiunt <u>procī</u>, 'et incolās īnsulae regere cupimus. ūnum nostrum statim
10 <u>ēlige</u>!'

Ulixēs īrātissimus erat et procōs avārōs occīdere cōnstituit. in ātrium vīllae suae vēnit et omnēs sagittīs hastīsque occīdit. tum, lacrimīs plūrimīs, post vīgintī annōs, uxōrem cārissimam tandem salutāvit Pēnelopam.

petō, -ere, petīvī = I seek	avārus, -a, -um = greedy
procus, -ī, m. = suitor	ātrium, -ī, n. = hall
vīlla, -ae, f. = house	lacrima, -ae, f. = tear
in mātrimōnium dūcere = to marry	annus, -ī, m. = year
ēligō, -ere = I choose	

1 Nausicaa, postquam Ulixem ad vīllam parentum suōrum dūxit (line 1). Where did Nausicaa take Ulysses?

2 ducem audācissimum diū audiēbat (lines 1–2). What did she do when she got there?

3 is rēgī dē plūrimīs perīculīs itineris nārrāvit auxiliumque petīvit (lines 2–3). What did Ulysses do when he met the king?

4 rēx Ulixem amābat et eī nāvem nautāsque dedit (line 3). How did the king react to Ulysses's request?

5 'nāvigāte ad īnsulam Ithacam' inquit 'et Graecum fortissimum ad uxōrem eius dūcite' (lines 4–5). What were the king's instructions to the sailors?

6 plūrimōs (line 6).

   (a) In which case is this word?

   (b) What form of which adjective is this word?

7 pulcherrimam (line 7).

   (a) In which case is this word?

   (b) What form of which adjective is this word?

8 eam (line 7).

   (a) What sort of word is this?

   (b) In which case is it?

   (c) Give the nominative singular masculine form.

9 mortuus (line 8). What is the connection between this Latin word and the English word **mortuary**?

10   nostrum (line 9).

   (a) What sort of word is this?

   (b) In which case is it?

   (c) Give its nominative plural form.

11   īrātissimus (line 11). Give the positive and comparative forms of this adjective.

12   vēnit (line 12). This verb means **he came**. How would you say in Latin **he will come**?

13   Ulixēs ... salutāvit (lines 11–13). Translate these lines.

Vocabulary 6

Latin	English
Prepositions	
ante + acc.	before
circum + acc.	around
inter + acc.	between, among
post + acc.	after
prō + abl.	on behalf of, in place of, in front of
propter + acc.	on account of
sine + abl.	without
sub + abl.	under
super + acc.	over
Verbs	
colligō, -ere, collēgī, collēctum	I collect
dēbeō, -ēre, dēbuī, dēbitum	I owe, ought
dēfendō, -ere, dēfendī, dēfēnsum	I defend
gerō, -ere, gessī, gestum	I carry on, wear
servō, -āre, -āvī, -ātum	I save
vulnerō, -āre, -āvī, -ātum	I wound

The amphitheatre

When Odysseus returned to Ithaca and found the suitors living in his house, the slaughter that he unleashed in the great hall was truly terrible. This story would have appealed to the bloodthirsty Romans, for whom slaughter was a popular form of entertainment. In amphitheatres such as the mighty Colosseum in Rome, which held 50,000 people, Romans would regularly watch fights between

> This topic is part of the Non-Linguistic Studies section of the ISEB syllabus.

gladiators or wild beasts. These might involve a secūtor, armed with a shield and sword, fighting against a rētiārius with a trident and a net. Or it might be a slave fighting off wild beasts. Whatever the spectacle, the arena would have been drenched in gore and had sand (harēna) sprinkled on it to soak up the blood.

Gladiators were trained by a lanista (trainer) whose job was to ensure a suitably gory spectacle, as can be seen in the picture below.

■ A Roman mosaic showing gladiators fighting, watched by their lanista (trainer)

Exercise 6.12

(a) (i) Tell the story of the homecoming of Odysseus.

(ii) What do you think Penelope felt when she was reunited with Odysseus after such a long time?

(b) (i) Give an account of a visit to a Roman amphitheatre.

(ii) Which form of entertainment in the modern world might be compared to the spectacles seen in the amphitheatre?

7 Hic, haec, hoc; ille, illa, illud

◯ Hic, haec, hoc

You have already met the demonstrative pronoun is, ea, id = that. In this chapter you're going to meet two other demonstrative pronouns: hic = this (near me) and ille = that (over there). We shall start with hic.

hic, haec, hoc = this (near me) [plural = these]		
	M	F	N
Nom.	hic	haec	hoc
Acc.	hunc	hanc	hoc
Gen.	huius	huius	huius
Dat.	huic*	huic	huic
Abl.	hōc	hāc	hōc
Nom.	hī	hae	haec
Acc.	hōs	hās	haec
Gen.	hōrum	hārum	hōrum
Dat.	hīs	hīs	hīs
Abl.	hīs	hīs	hīs

* This word is a diphthong, and should be pronounced as one syllable.

In the same way that is, ea, id can be used to mean he, she or it, so too hic, haec, hoc is often used in this way.

E.g.   rēgīna virum sapientem amat. **hic** poēta clārissimus erat.

The queen loved the wise man. **He** was a very famous poet.

Be sure not to confuse hic = this with hīc = here. It should always be clear from the context, though of course the words are pronounced differently.

Exercise 7.1

Translate into English:

1. hic agricola
2. haec fēmina
3. hoc flūmen
4. hī mīlitēs
5. hae uxōrēs
6. haec vulnera
7. huius nāvis
8. huic sorōrī
9. hārum partium
10. hārum mulierum

Exercise 7.2

Give the Latin for:

1. This town (nom.)
2. These girls (acc.)
3. Of this mother
4. For this leader
5. Of these citizens
6. In this city
7. Towards this island
8. Near this wall
9. Concerning these dangers
10. This wine

Exercise 7.3

Translate into English:

1. ad oppidum cum hōc servō festīnābam.
2. haec fēmina uxor est ducis nostrī.
3. dā cibum huic mīlitī!
4. haec flūmina altiōra sunt quam ea.
5. fīlium huius virī occīdī.
6. hic cīvis in eō templō dormiēbat.
7. hī frātrēs in eā urbe habitābant.
8. nōnne hanc ancillam amās?
9. vīnum huic virō dare cupiō.
10. perīcula hōrum bellōrum maxima sunt.

Exercise 7.4

Study the following passage and answer the questions below.

Perseus – his early years

Perseus erat fīlius Iovis, omnium deōrum maximī. rēx Argōrum, Ācrisius
nōmine, erat huius puerī avus nec tamen eum amābat. nam propter
ōrāculum puerum magnopere timēbat et eum occīdere cupiēbat. rēx
igitur saevus Perseum, etiamtum īnfantem, rapuit et in arcam cum mātre
5 Danaē posuit. tum arcam in mare iēcit.
   Iuppiter tamen haec omnia vīdit et fīlium suum servāre cōnstituit. itaque
arcam ad īnsulam Serīphum dūxit. Danaē autem et fīlius eius ad lītus tūtī
advēnērunt. rēx huius īnsulae erat Polydectēs. hic mox eam mātrem
pulcherrimam amābat et in mātrimōnium dūcere cupiēbat.
10 per multōs annōs Danaē et Perseus in hāc īnsulā habitābant. Perseus
rēgem nōn amābat nec mātrem suam uxōrem virī crūdēlis esse cupiēbat.
Polydectēs igitur puerum dīmittere cōnstituit.

Iuppiter, Iovis, m. = Jupiter	Danaē (acc. Danaēn, gen.
Argī, -ōrum, m. pl. = Argos	Danaēs, abl. Danaē), f. =
(a town in Greece)	Danae
avus, -ī, m. = grandfather	Serīphus, -ī, f. = Seriphos
nec tamen = but ... not	lītus, lītoris, n. = shore
ōrāculum, -ī, n. = oracle	in mātrimōnium dūcō = I
etiamtum = while still	marry
īnfans, īnfantis, c. = little	annus, -ī, m. = year
child	nec = and ... not
rapiō, -ere, rapuī = I seize	dimittō, -ere = I send away
arca, -ae, f. = chest	

1 Perseus erat fīlius Iovis, omnium deōrum maximī (line 1). Who was Perseus?

2 rēx Argōrum, Ācrisius nōmine, erat huius puerī avus (lines 1–2). Who was
   Acrisius?

3 nam propter ōrāculum puerum magnopere timēbat et eum occīdere
   cupiēbat (lines 2–3). Why did Acrisius want to kill Perseus?

4 rēx igitur ... in mare iēcit (lines 3–5). How did Acrisius plan to get rid of
   Perseus?

5 haec (line 6). In which case is this word?

6 huius (line 8). With which word does this agree?

7 hāc (line 10). In which case is this word?

8 posuit (line 5). Give the 1st person singular of the present tense of this verb.

9 pulcherrimam (line 9). Which form of which adjective is this?

10 Translate the passage into English.

◯ ille, illa, illud

The other demonstrative pronoun we are going to learn in this chapter is ille, illa, illud. Whereas hic, haec, hoc means this (near me), ille, illa, illud means that (over there).

ille, illa, illud = that (over there) [plural = those]			
	M	F	N
Nom.	ille	illa	illud
Acc.	illum	illam	illud
Gen.	illius	illius	illius
Dat.	illī	illī	illī
Abl.	illō	illā	illō
Nom.	illī	illae	illa
Acc.	illōs	illās	illa
Gen.	illōrum	illārum	illōrum
Dat.	illīs	illīs	illīs
Abl.	illīs	illīs	illīs

Exercise 7.5

Translate into English:

1 illōrum agricolārum

2 illa bella

3 illius fēminae

4 ab illō magistrō

5 illārum ancillārum

6 illī mīlitēs

7 illae uxōrēs

8 illud flūmen

9 ille incola

10 cum illīs sociīs

Exercise 7.6

Translate into English:

1. ubi est illa fēmina?

2. hic servus melior est quam ille.

3. ille cīvis laetissimus est.

4. nōnne illam mulierem vīdistī?

5. in illud oppidum ambulābant.

6. dōnum illī poētae dedit.

7. fīlius illius rēgis audācissimus est.

8. hic magister omnēs puerōs puellāsque ex oppidō dūcet.

9. num pugnābitis cum illō virō?

10. sagittās in illud flūmen iēcērunt.

Go further

Using is, hic and ille

1. Hic and ille work just like is, ea, id in that, when not used in agreement with a noun, they mean 'he', 'she' or 'it'.

   E.g. mīles hunc interfēcit = The soldier killed him (i.e. *this man here*).

2. Ille and hic may be used like 'the former ... the latter'. In such cases, ille means the former (because further away in the sentence!) and hic means the latter (because nearer).

   E.g. Mārcus agricolam vīdit. ille īrātus erat, hic dormiēbat = Marcus saw the farmer. The *former* (i.e. Marcus) was angry, the *latter* (i.e. the farmer) was asleep.

3. The normal word to use for him, her, them, etc., is is, ea, id, unless you are clearly referring to someone or something near to you, in which case use hic, haec, hoc, or far away in the distance, in which case use ille, illa, illud.

Exercise 7.7

Study the information above about hic and ille. Then translate into Latin:

1. These soldiers were attacking that city.

2. We will read these books now.

3. Marcus and Brutus are soldiers. The former is brave and the latter is very strong.

4 Those kings had ruled this city.

5 All the citizens feared that danger.

6 He will place these gifts in that temple.

7 We were watching those farmers (over there).

8 That poet did not like him.

9 Why did you not depart from that country?

10 He was carrying the food through the streets of that city.

Exercise 7.8

Study the following passage and answer the questions below.

The Gauls enter Rome, 390 BC

Gallī autem urbem intrāvērunt quod incolae eōs timēbant. fēminae et
iuvenēs in montem Capitōlīnum fūgerant sed senēs in forō sedēbant.
Gallī in forum ambulāvērunt et diū eōs spectābant. senēs Rōmānī nihil
faciēbant. tandem Gallus ad senem Rōmānum appropinquāvit et barbam
5 eius carpsit. is īrātus erat et clāmāvit. statim Gallus eum occīdit et
comitēs eius omnēs Rōmānōs occīdērunt. mīlitēs autem nōn invēnērunt
quod illī in monte cum fēminīs manēbant.

diū Rōmānī in monte manēbant. tandem Gallī montem ascendērunt.
mīlitēs Rōmānī eōs nōn audīvērunt. ānserēs tamen, sacrī deae Iūnōnī, in
10 monte aderant. hī Gallōs audīvērunt et ululāvērunt. mīlitēs sē
excitāvērunt et hostēs dē monte pepulērunt.

Capitōlīnus, -a, -um = Capitoline	ānser, ānseris, m. = goose
forum, -ī, n. = forum	Iūnō, Iūnōnis, f. = Juno
carpō, -ere, carpsī = I pluck	ululō, -āre, -āvī = I screech
ascendō, -ere, ascendī = I go up	sē excitō, -āre, -āvī = I wake up
	pellō, -ere, pepulī = I drive

1 Gallī autem urbem intrāvērunt quod incolae eōs timēbant (line 1). Why were
the Gauls able to enter the city?

2 fēminae et iuvenēs in montem Capitōlīnum ascenderant sed senēs in forō
sedēbant (lines 1–2). How did the old men's reaction to the arrival of the
Gauls differ from that of the women and young men?

3 Gallī in forum ambulāvērunt et diū eōs spectābant (line 3). How did the Gauls behave when they entered the forum?

4 senēs Rōmānī nihil faciēbant (lines 3–4). What did the old men do?

5 tandem Gallus … is īrātus erat (lines 4–5). What was it that angered the Roman?

6 statim Gallus eum occīdit et comitēs eius omnēs Rōmānōs occīdērunt (lines 5–6). What happened to the old Roman men after this?

7 mīlitēs autem nōn invēnērunt quod illī in monte cum fēminīs manēbant (lines 6–7). How did the soldiers escape this fate?

8 manēbant (line 7). This verb means **they were remaining**. How would you say in Latin **they will remain**?

9 audīvērunt (line 9).

   (a) What is the subject of this verb?

   (b) What is the object of this verb?

10 Rōmānī (line 9). With which Latin word does this adjective agree?

11 deae (line 9). In which case is this word?

12 monte (line 10).

   (a) In which case is this word?

   (b) Why is it in this case?

13 hī (line 10).

   (a) In which case and number is this word?

   (b) Give its nominative singular masculine form.

14 audīvērunt (line 10).

   (a) In which tense is this verb?

   (b) Give the present infinitive of this verb.

   (c) Put this verb into the future tense, keeping the person and number the same.

15 Translate the passage into English.

Vocabulary 7

Latin	English
Verbs	
līberō, -āre, -āvī, -ātum	I free
nārrō, -āre, -āvī, -ātum	I tell
Adverbs	
celeriter	quickly
crās	tomorrow
forte	by chance
frūstrā	in vain
herī	yesterday
nunc	now
posteā	afterwards
quam	how
quoque	also
tum	then
Conjunctions	
antequam	before
nam	for
postquam	after

Army camps

The Romans suffered a number of humiliations at the hands of the Gauls in the early years of their history, as the story above shows. But as their power increased, so did the efficiency of their military organisation. One important feature of this can be seen in the way they built their camps. These always followed a common plan, built on a grid system, which meant that wherever the camp (castra) was built, the soldiers always knew their way around it.

A typical camp was rectangular in shape and occupied one square kilometre. Around the perimeter they dug a ditch (fossa), and the earth from this was piled up to form a rampart (agger), on top of which they built a palisade (vallum) out of wooden stakes.

In each of the four sides of the camp there was a gate, for easy exit, and the gates were linked by two main roads. Where these roads met, in the middle of the camp, was the main headquarters (principia).

This topic is part of the Non-Linguistic Studies section of the ISEB syllabus.

Roman soldiers carried with them, as part of their normal equipment, digging tools and stakes to allow them to build these camps wherever they went. But in some places these temporary structures became permanent. The wood was replaced by stone, and more elaborate buildings grew up inside the walls, such as temples and bath houses. Outside the walls of the camp, a town would grow up where the families of the soldiers would live, and many towns around the empire developed which were clearly based on these once temporary Roman camps. A very obvious clue to this may be seen in the name of many British towns: where you see the word -chester (castra), as in Winchester, Rochester, or even Chester itself, you can be sure that once a Roman camp thrived on that site.

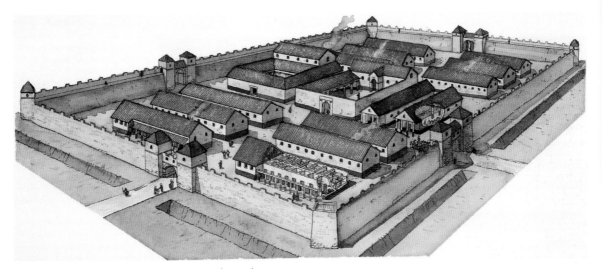

■ An artist's impression of a Roman camp (castra)

Exercise 7.9

(a) (i) Tell the story of how Perseus came to be living on the island of Seriphos.

   (ii) Why do you think King Polydectes wanted to get rid of Perseus?

(b) (i) Describe a typical army camp. Draw a diagram to illustrate your answer.

   (ii) Why do you think army camps were always built on the same design?

8 possum; eō; reflexive pronouns

◯ possum = I am able

A very useful compound of the verb sum is the verb possum = I am able. This is a combination of the adjective potis = able and sum, and it goes as follows:

possum, posse, potuī = I am able	
Present	**Imperfect**
possum	poteram
potes	poterās
potest	poterat
possumus	poterāmus
potestis	poterātis
possunt	poterant
Future	**Perfect**
poterō	potuī
poteris	potuistī
poterit	potuit
poterimus	potuimus
poteritis	potuistis
poterunt	potuērunt

1 As you can see, the first three tenses are simply the verb sum preceded by either pot- or pos-. The present infinitive posse = 'to be able' is a squashed result of pos- and esse.
2 A very common way of translating possum is with the English word 'can'.
E.g. possum cantāre = I can sing.

Exercise 8.1

Translate into English:

1 legere possunt.

2 scrībere potest.

3 dormīre potestis.

4 nāvigāre nōn poteram.

5 pugnāre poterāmus.

6 vidēre potuerant.

7 venīre poterō.

8 labōrāre posse.

9 nōnne currere potes?

10 effugere nōn potuit.

Exercise 8.2

Translate into Latin:

1 We can sing.

2 You (pl.) can read.

3 She can't see.

4 I was not able to fight.

5 We were able to escape.

6 Are you (sing.) able to sail?

7 We had not been able to come.

8 To be able.

9 The slaves were able to work.

10 They were not able to fight.

Exercise 8.3

Translate into English:

1 hī mīlitēs eōs cīvēs superāre nōn poterant.

2 illam deam vidēre nōn poterimus.

3 ego trāns illud mare cum multīs comitibus meīs nāvigāre poteram.

4 nōnne incolae illīus oppidī templum maius aedificāre possunt?

5 magister puerōs peiōrēs regere nōn poterat.

6 fēmina ancillam meliōrem vidēre nōn potuerat.

7 puella parva aquam in oppidum portāre nōn potuerat.

8 paucī virī montem maximum vidēre poterunt.

9 vōcem mulieris pulcherrimae audīre nōn poterātis.

10 iuvenis cum senibus cantāre poterit.

Study the following passage and answer the questions below:

The story of Regulus, 249 BC

ōlim Rōmānī cum <u>Poenīs</u> pugnābant. dux autem Rōmānōrum, nōmine
Rēgulus, multās <u>victōriās pepererat</u>; <u>Carthāginem</u> tamen nōn cēperat.
Rēgulus igitur mīlitibus 'nōnne Rōmānī' inquit 'hostēs semper
superābunt? omnem Ītaliam nōs Rōmānī nunc regimus. īnsulam Siciliam
5 regimus. hanc urbem quoque capiēmus et crās cibum vīnumque ibi
cōnsūmēmus.'

diū <u>pugnātum est</u>, sed tandem <u>Poenī</u> Rōmānōs superāvērunt. plūrimōs
Rōmānōs occīdērunt; Rēgulum cēpērunt, in urbem dūxērunt. post hoc
<u>lēgātōs</u> ad cīvēs Rōmānōs mīsērunt. inter hōs erat Rēgulus. antequam
10 eum mīsērunt, <u>Poenī</u> ducem Rōmānum <u>pācem</u> rogāre iussērunt; eī*
tamen nōn <u>persuāsērunt</u>.

Rēgulus, ubi in urbem vēnit, īn <u>forum</u> Rōmānum ambulāvit et <u>prō</u> bellō
<u>disseruit</u>. 'arma <u>Pūnica</u> nōn timeō' inquit '<u>nec</u> <u>pācem</u> habēre cum
hostibus cupiō.' ubi omnia haec dīxit ad hostēs <u>revēnit</u>. illī autem ducem
15 fortissimum <u>crūdēliter</u> occīdērunt.

*Some verbs in Latin take an indirect object in the dative case, rather than a direct one in the
accusative. Common examples of this are crēdō = I believe and persuadeō = I persuade.

Poenī, -ōrum, m. pl. = Carthaginians	forum, -ī, n. = forum
victōriam pariō, -ere, peperī = I win a victory	prō (here) = in support of
	disserō, -ere, disseruī = I speak
Carthāgō, -inis, f. = Carthage	arma, -ōrum, n. pl. = arms
pugnātum est = the battle raged	Pūnicus, -a, -um = Carthaginian
lēgātus, -ī, m. = ambassador	nec = and … not, nor
pāx, pācis, f. = peace	reveniō, -īre, revēnī = I return
persuādeō, -ēre, persuāsī (+ dat.) = I persuade	crūdēliter = cruelly

1 dux autem Rōmānōrum … nōn cēperat (lines 1–2). In what way had Regulus
not been entirely successful as a general?

2 'nōnne Rōmānī' inquit … nunc regimus' (lines 3–5). How did Regulus try to
inspire his soldiers with these words?

3 'crās hanc urbem quoque capiēmus et ibi cibum vīnumque cōnsūmēmus' (lines 5–6). What did Regulus tell his soldiers that they would soon be doing in the city?

4 plūrimōs (line 7).

    (a) What sort of word is this?

    (b) Give its positive and comparative forms.

5 hoc (line 8).

    (a) What sort of word is this?

    (b) Give its nominative singular masculine form.

6 eum (line 10).

    (a) What sort of word is this?

    (b) Give its nominative singular masculine form.

7 rogāre (line 10). Which form of which verb is this?

8 iussērunt (line 10).

    (a) In which tense is this verb?

    (b) Give the 1st person singular of its present tense.

9 urbem (line 12). What is the connection between this noun and the English word **urban**?

10 hostibus (line 14).

    (a) In which case is this noun?

    (b) Why is this case used?

11 omnia haec (line 14).

    (a) In which case are these words?

    (b) Put these words into the genitive plural, keeping the gender the same.

12 Translate the passage into English.

eō = I go

Another irregular verb to learn is eō = I go. It is only really irregular in the present tense, although the perfect is a bit peculiar. The iī (rather than the īvī) forms are the more common, so take care over the contracted forms īstī and īstis.

eo, ire, iī (or īvī), itum = I go	
Present	**Imperfect**
eō	ībam
īs	ībās
it	ībat
īmus	ībāmus
ītis	ībātis
eunt	ībant
Future	**Perfect**
ībō	iī
ībis	īstī
ībit	iit
ībimus	iimus
ībitis	īstis
ībunt	iērunt
Imperatives	
Sing.	ī
Pl.	īte

Compounds of eō

There are a number of very useful compounds of eō:

exeō = I go out

ineō = I go in, enter

redeō = I go back, return

trānseō = I go across, cross

pereō = I perish, die

Exercise 8.5

Write out the following tenses, complete with meanings:

1 Present tense of exeō

2 Future tense of ineō

3 Imperfect tense of redeō

4 Perfect tense of trānseō

5 Pluperfect tense of pereō

Exercise 8.6

Translate into English:

1 cīvēs celeriter ex oppidō exībunt.

2 omnēs in agrōs inībimus.

3 puerī puellaeque ab īnsulā redībant.

4 ancillae circum templa ībant.

5 num servī flūmen sine dominō trānsībant?

6 ad urbem magnam, ō iuvenēs, redīte!

7 in bellō magnō plūrimī mīlitēs perierant.

8 nōnne mēcum flūmen altum trānsībitis?

9 parentēs nostrī in oppidum redībant.

10 rex vester in proelium numquam init.

Exercise 8.7

Translate into Latin:

1 We shall go into the fields.

2 They were crossing the great river.

3 I had gone into the temple.

4 You (pl.) will not perish in that war.

5 We have returned from the city.

6 She is going out into the street.

7 Why are you (pl.) crossing the mountains?

8 They will return from the island.

9 They never go out from the town.

10 She has returned to her fatherland.

◯ Reflexive pronouns

The reflexive pronoun in Latin is sē. It works in the same way as in French, where we see phrases such as 'il s'appelle' (he calls himself), 'il se lave' (he washes himself), etc. It has no nominative or vocative form, and the singular and plural are the same:

Acc.	sē
Gen.	suī
Dat.	sibi
Abl.	sē

Reflexive pronouns are very rare in the genitive, and in the ablative are usually found in the phrase sēcum = with himself/herself/themselves.

E.g.   dominus sē necāvit = The king killed himself.

poēta sibī cantābat = The poet was singing to himself.

mīlitēs gladiōs sēcum portābant = The soldiers carried swords with them.

Exercise 8.8

Translate into English:

1 rēx gladiō sē necāvit.

2 cīvēs gladiīs sē necāvērunt.

3 dux fortis sē vulnerāvit.

4 mīlitēs sē vulnerāvērunt.

5 iuvenis ā rēge sē līberābit.

6 cīvēs sagittīs et gladiīs sē dēfendēbant.

7 agricola in hōc agrō semper sibī cantat.

8 senex verba poētārum sibī dīcēbat.

9 servī cibum vīnumque sēcum portābant.

10 fēmina in templō subitō sē occīdit.

Exercise 8.9

Translate into English:

Perseus and Medusa

Polydectēs autem Perseum <u>dīmittere</u> cōnstituerat. iuvenem igitur ad sē
vocāvit et haec dīxit: 'nunc tempus est tibi,' inquit, '<u>fāmam</u> maximam
<u>quaerere</u>. <u>abī</u>, et caput Medūsae cape!'
    Perseus, ubi haec audīvit, ab īnsulā discessit et Medūsam <u>quaerēbat</u>.
<u>prīmō</u> ad <u>Graeās</u>, Medūsae sorōrēs, <u>pervēnit</u>. hae ūnum <u>modŏ</u> <u>oculum</u>
5 inter sē habēbant nec iuvenem <u>adiuvāre</u> cupiēbant. ab hīs tamen <u>tālāria</u> et
<u>galeam</u> <u>magicam</u> accēpit. inde Apollō et Minerva eī <u>falcem</u> et <u>speculum</u>
dedērunt. Perseus <u>tālāria</u> <u>induit</u>, in caelum <u>volābat</u>, et deōrum auxiliō ad
locum ubi <u>Gorgonēs</u> habitābant advēnit. <u>Gorgonēs</u> <u>mōnstra</u> saeva erant:
capita eārum <u>anguibus</u> <u>contēcta</u> erant et <u>sī quis</u> eās cōnspexerat, <u>lapis</u>
10 statim fiēbat. Perseus tamen <u>tergum</u> <u>vertit</u> et Medūsam īn <u>speculō</u>
spectāvit. tum caput eius <u>falce</u> <u>abscīdit</u> et discessit.

dīmittō, -ere, dīmīsī = I send away
fama, -ae, f. = fame
quaerō, -ere, quaesīvī = I look for
prīmō = at first
Graeae, -ārum, f. pl. = the Graeae
perveniō, -īre, pervēnī = I arrive at
modo = only
oculus, -ī, m. = eye
adiuvō, -āre = I help
tālāria, -um, n. pl. = winged
sandals
galea, -ae, f. = helmet
magicus, -a, -um = magic
falx, falcis, f. = sickle
speculum, -ī, n. = mirror
induō, -ere, induī = I put on
volō, -āre = I fly
Gorgō, -onis, f. = Gorgon
mōnstrum, -ī, n. = monster
anguis, -is, c. = snake
contēctus, -a, -um = covered
sī quis = if anyone, i.e. whoever
fiō, -ere = I become
abscīdō, -ere, abscīdī = I cut off

■ A woodcut artist's impression of Perseus, after he has killed
Medusa by cutting off her head

Vocabulary 8

Latin	English
Adjectives	
audāx, audācis	bold
crūdēlis, -e	cruel
difficilis, -e	difficult
facilis, -e	easy
fēlīx, fēlīcis	fortunate
fortis, -e	brave, strong
ingēns, ingentis	huge
nōbilis, -e	noble
omnis, -e	all, every
sapiēns, sapientis	wise
trīstis, -e	sad
Pronouns	
hic, haec, hoc	this
ille, illa, illud	that
is, ea, id	that
sē	himself, herself, itself, themselves

Baths and clothing

The Romans loved baths. Rich people had baths in their own homes, but everyone loved to go to the baths to relax, meet friends and exchange gossip.

A typical bath house was built on the same basic layout. The heating came from an under-floor heating system called a hypocaust. Bathers would move from the apodyterium (changing room) to the tepidārium (warm room), then the caldārium (hot room) and finally, to cool down, the frīgidārium (cold room). They might enjoy a massage, where a slave would scrape them down with a strigilis (scraper), or a game of ball in the palaestra (exercise yard).

This topic is part of the Non-Linguistic Studies section of the ISEB syllabus.

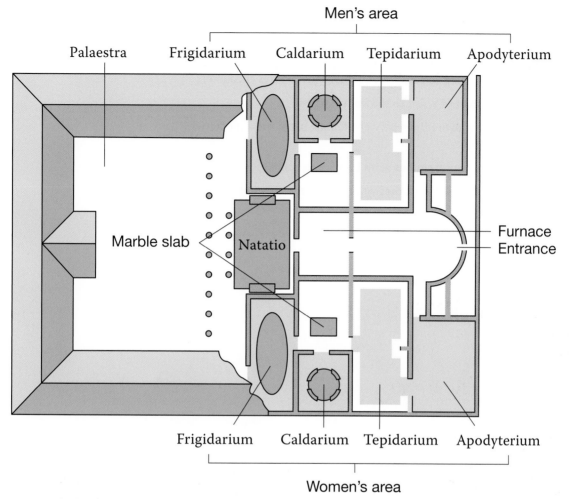

Men's area

Palaestra   Frigidarium   Caldarium   Tepidarium   Apodyterium

Marble slab   Natatio

Furnace
Entrance

Frigidarium   Caldarium   Tepidarium   Apodyterium

Women's area

■ Roman baths

Back in the apodyterium, the bather would put their clothes back on. Roman men wore a plain tunic (tūnica) with a belt at the waist. Knights wore a tunic with two thin purple stripes down the front, and senators, the most important citizens, wore one with a broad purple stripe, the tūnica lāticlāvia. Over the tunic all men wore a toga, the toga virilis, apart from senators and priests, who wore a toga with a broad purple stripe around its edge, the toga praetēxta. Women wore a tunic and a dress (stola), with a cloak (palla) over the top. Both men and women wore sandals (soleae). Children wore a necklace around their necks called a bulla, and Roman boys wore a toga praetēxta until their 16th birthday, when they came of age and put on the toga virilis.

Exercise 8.10

(a) (i) Tell the story of how Perseus overcame the Gorgon Medusa.

   (ii) What qualities did Perseus have to display during this encounter?

(b) (i) Give an account of a visit to the Roman baths.

   (ii) What similarities are there between Roman baths and a modern leisure centre?

(c) (i) Describe the typical clothes worn by a Roman family.

   (ii) In what ways were the clothes worn by Romans different from those worn by people today?

9 Concessive clauses; prohibitions

Concessive clauses

These are introduced by conjunctions meaning **although** or **even if**.

E.g.   quamquam festīnās, servum nōn capiēs.

Although you are hurrying, you will not catch the slave.

E.g.   puerī, quamquam diū dormīverant, fessī erant.

Although the boys had slept for a long time, they were tired.

Exercise 9.1

Translate into English:

1   mīlitēs, quamquam fortiter pugnābant, hostēs nōn superāvērunt.

2   quamquam fēminae fessae erant, ad urbem ambulābant.

3   flūmen, quamquam altissimum erat, trānsīre cupiēbāmus.

4   cīvēs illum poētam, quamquam pessimus erat, diū laudābant.

5   eum magistrum, quamquam īrātissimus erat, nōn timēbāmus.

6   in proelium, quamquam hostēs saevissimī erant, nōs festīnāvimus.

7   illōs virōs, quamquam fortissimī erant, nōn amābant hae mulierēs.

8   nautae, quamquam mare timēbant, ad īnsulam celeriter nāvigābant.

9   illum montem, quamquam altissimus est, trānsīre cupiēbat.

10 rēgīnam, quamquam aderam, vidēre nōn poteram.

Exercise 9.2

Revision of subordinate clauses. Translate into English:

1   rēx, ubi servōs miserōs cōnspexit, eōs ad urbem suam mīsit.

2   Rōmānī, quod multōs servōs in oppidum dūxerant, laetissimī erant.

3   fīlia mīlitis, ubi agricolam cōnspexit, mūrōs altōs trānsiit.

4 iuvenēs, quamquam in urbem inīre cupiēbant, in agrīs diū manēbant.

5 hī virī, quod uxōrēs pulcherrimās cupiēbant, ad urbem maximam iter fēcērunt.

6 trāns hoc flūmen, quamquam altius quam illud est, trānsīre cōnstituimus.

7 quamquam fessī erant, mīlitēs fortissimī cum hostibus pugnābant.

8 ancilla aquam et cibum dominō suō, quamquam eum timēbat, dare cupiēbat.

9 incolae, quod multa vulnera accēperant, ē proeliō discēssērunt.

10 senēs, quod sapientissimī erant, multa verba iuvenibus dīcēbant.

Prohibitions

Negative commands, or prohibitions, are expressed in Latin by nōlī/ nōlīte + the infinitive. If you are addressing one person, use nōlī. If you are addressing more than one, use nōlīte.

E.g.   nōlī currere, puer!

Don't run, boy!

E.g.   nōlīte currere, puellae!

Don't run, girls!

Exercise 9.3

Translate into English:

1 nōlī occīdere illum virum!

2 nōlīte fugere ab illō agricolā!

3 nōlī hunc cibum cōnsūmere!

4 nōlīte illud flūmen trānsīre!

5 nōlīte timēre eōs senēs!

6 nōlī legere hunc librum, magister!

7 nōlīte, puerī audācēs, in viam ruere!

8 nōlī dōnum illud senī miserō trādere!

9 nōlīte equōs fessōs ex agrō dūcere!

10 nōlī, poēta, ab hāc īnsulā discēdere!

Exercise 9.4

Translate into Latin:

1 Don't sing, boy!

2 Don't sing, boys!

3 Don't depart, citizens!

4 Don't sleep, young man!

5 Don't do that, slave-girls!

6 Don't say these things, slave!

7 Enter the temple, poet!

8 Don't enter the temple, poet!

9 O king, don't praise the queen's children!

10 Don't remain here, inhabitants!

Exercise 9.5

Study the following passage and answer the questions below.

Perseus and Andromeda

Perseus, ubi ē terrā <u>Gorgonum</u> discessit, in <u>fīnēs Aethiopum</u> advēnit. ibi
rēx, nōmine Cēpheus, incolās regēbat. Neptūnus autem, quod rēx eum
<u>offenderat</u>, ad incolās <u>mōnstrum</u> saevissimum mīserat. hoc ē marī <u>cōtīdiē</u>
veniēbat et hominēs miserōs cōnsūmēbat.

5   Cēpheus igitur <u>ōrāculum cōnsulere</u> cōnstituit et haec verba audīvit:
'fīliam tuam' inquit '<u>mōnstrō</u> trāde!' fīlia autem rēgis, nōmine Andromeda,
puella pulcherrima erat. Cēpheus eam magnopere amābat <u>nec mōnstrō</u> trādere
cupiēbat. cīvēs tamen, quamquam puellam amābant, ē perīculō effugere
cupiēbant. '<u>nōlī neglegere</u> verba deī', inquiunt. 'fīliam tuam ad mare portā!'

10   rēx miser, quod cīvēs suōs servāre cupiēbat, fīliam ad <u>lītus</u> dūxit et ad
<u>rūpem adligāvit</u>. omnēs perterritī spectābant et <u>mōnstrum</u> exspectābant.
subitō Perseus advēnit et puellam cōnspexit. <u>mōnstrum</u> ad eam ē marī
appropinquābat, sed iuvenis, postquam <u>tālāria induit</u>, <u>prōvolāvit</u> et oppugnāvit.
gladiō caput mōnstrī vulnerāvit et mox mare <u>sanguine</u> rubēbat. <u>mōnstrum</u>

15 <u>ululāvit</u> et in <u>undās</u> sē <u>mērsit</u>. Perseus autem Andromedam servāverat.

Gorgō, Gorgonis, f. = Gorgon	rūpēs, -is, f. = cliff
fīnēs, fīnum, m. pl. = territory	adligō, -āre, -āvī = I tie up
Aethiopēs, -um, m. pl. = the Ethiopians	tālāria, -um, n. pl. = winged sandals
offendō, -ere, offendī = I offend	induō, -ere, induī = I put on
mōnstrum, -ī, n. = monster	prōvolō, -āre, -āvī = I fly forward
cōtīdiē = every day	sanguis, -inis, m. = blood
ōrāculum, -ī, n. = oracle	rubeō, -ēre, rubuī = I am red
cōnsulō, -ere = I consult	ululō, -āre, -āvī = I howl
nec = and ... not	unda, -ae, f. = wave
neglegō, -ere = I neglect	mergō, -ere, mērsī = I immerse
lītus, lītoris, n. = shore	

1 Perseus, ubi ē terrā Gorgonum discessit, in fīnēs Aethiopum advēnit (line 1). What are we told about Perseus in these lines?

2 ibi rēx, nōmine Cēpheus, incolās regēbat (lines 1–2). Who was Cepheus?

3 Neptūnus autem, quod rēx eum offenderat, ad incolās mōnstrum saevissimum mīserat (lines 2–3). Why did Neptune send a monster?

4 hoc ē marī cōtīdiē veniēbat et hominēs miserōs cōnsūmēbat (lines 3–4). What did this monster do every day?

5 cōnstituit (line 5). In which tense is this verb?

6 haec verba (line 5). In which case are these words?

7 mōnstrō (line 6). In which case is this word?

8 pulcherrima (line 7). What form of this adjective is this?

9 trādere (line 7). What form of this verb is this?

10 quamquam puellam amābant (line 8). What type of clause is this?

11 'nōlī neglegere verba deī' (line 9).

   (a) What construction is this?

   (b) What would the word nōlī become if the citizens were speaking to more than one person?

12 mare (line 9). In which case is this word?

13 portā! (line 9).

   (a) What form of this verb is this?

   (b) What is the connection between this word and the English word **portable**?

14 rēx ... servāverat (lines 10–15). Translate these lines into English.

> ## A word on compound verbs
>
> Many verbs in Latin are called compound verbs, because they are made up of a prefix (usually a preposition) followed by a simple verb. The various compounds of eō are a good example of this (redeō, ineō, exeō, etc.). One thing to note with many of these verbs is that the relevant preposition is often, but not always, repeated in the sentence.
>
> E.g.   ex oppidō exeunt = They go out of the town.
>
>   in flūmen ineunt = They go into the river.

Exercise 9.6

Translate into English:

1 cīvēs ex urbe celeriter exeunt.

2 dux noster proelium fortiter inībat.

3 amīcī meī ad īnsulam mēcum redībunt.

4 omnēs fēminae in templum magnum inībant.

5 mīlitēs īnsulam cum duce fortī trānsiērunt.

6 puer miser in monte altō periit.

7 mox ille senex in hoc oppidum redībit.

8 crās mīlitēs fortēs in proelium redībunt.

9 servī et ancillae templum cum dominō iniērunt.

10 equus fessus ex flūmine altō exīre nōn poterat.

Exercise 9.7

Translate into Latin:

1 He will not cross the big sea.

2 They go into the smallest temple.

3 We will go back to our fatherland.

4 I have gone out from the very big town.

5 All the worst citizens have perished.

6 She had gone back to her mother.

7 You (sing.) were going across the angry farmer's field.

8 You (pl.) will not go into the city.

9 The young men have returned to the island.

10 They had not gone out of the very small temple.

Study the following passage and answer the questions below.

Perseus gets his revenge – twice

Perseus, postquam <u>mōnstrum</u> occīdit, Andromedam ā <u>rūpe</u> <u>līberāvit</u>. ea
laetissima erat et celeriter ad patrem rediit. rēx fīliam suam Perseō in
<u>mātrimōnium</u> dedit et paucōs <u>annōs</u>* iuvenis et uxor eius in eā terrā
habitābant. Perseus tamen mātrem suam iterum vidēre magnopere
5 cupiēbat et ad īnsulam Seriphum cum Andromedā rediit. mātrem diū
<u>quaerēbat</u> <u>nec tamen</u> eam invenīre poterat. tandem ad templum Diānae
advēnit. hīc fēmina misera, quod rēgem timēbat, sē <u>cēlābat</u>.

Perseus īrātus erat et ad <u>rēgiam</u> rēgis festīnāvit. in <u>ātrium</u> cucurrit et ibi
virum <u>superbum</u> vīdit. Polydectēs, ubi Perseum cōnspexit, effugere
10 <u>temptāvit</u>, sed frūstrā. iuvenis enim rēgī pessimō caput Gorgonis ostendit
et eum <u>lapideum</u> fēcit.

posteā Perseus cum uxōre suā ad <u>Ācrisī</u> urbem rediit. hic, propter
<u>ōrāculum</u>, <u>etiamtum</u> illum timēbat et ab eā terrā in urbem Lārissam fūgit.
<u>fātum</u> tamen nēmō <u>vītāre</u> potest. rēx enim Lārissae, post paucōs <u>annōs</u>,
15 <u>lūdōs</u> magnōs <u>facere</u> cōnstituit. nūntiōs in omnēs partēs Graeciae mīsit et
ex omnibus urbibus multī iuvenēs <u>convēnērunt</u>. in <u>numerō</u> eōrum aderat
Perseus et, ubi <u>discum</u> iēcit, <u>avum</u> suum occīdit. senex enim inter
<u>spectātōrēs</u> stābat et <u>discus</u> in eōs forte <u>volāvit</u>.

*A period of time is expressed in Latin by the accusative case: 'for a few years'.

mōnstrum, -ī, n. = monster	Ācrisius, -ī, m. = Acrisius (Perseus's grandfather)
rūpēs, -is, f. = cliff	ōrāculum, -ī, n. = oracle
līberō, -āre, -āvī = I free	etiamtum = still
mātrimōnium, -ī, n. = marriage	fātum, -ī, n. = fate
annus, -ī, m. = year	vītō, -āre = I avoid
quaerō, -ere = I look for	lūdōs faciō = I hold some games
nec tamen = but ... not	conveniō, -īre = I come together
cēlō, -āre = I hide	numerus, -ī, m. = number
rēgia, -ae, f. = palace	discus, -ī, m. = discus
ātrium, -ī, n. = hall	avus, -ī, m. = grandfather
superbus, -a, -um = proud	spectātor, -ōris, c. = spectator
temptō, -āre = I try	volō, -āre = I fly
lapideus = (made) of stone	

1 Perseus, postquam mōnstrum occīdit, Andromedam ā rūpe līberāvit
   (line 1). When did Perseus free Andromeda?

2 ea laetissima erat et celeriter ad patrem rediit (lines 1–2). What mood was
   she in and what did she do once she had been freed?

3 rēx fīliam suam Perseō in mātrimōnium dedit (lines 2–3). How did the king
   reward Perseus for his bravery?

4 Perseus tamen … cum Andromedā rediit (lines 4–5). Why did Perseus and
   Andromeda leave her home?

5 mātrem diū quaerēbat nec tamen eam invenīre poterat (lines 5–6). What
   did Perseus do when he got to Seriphos and with what success?

6 tandem ad templum … sē cēlābat (lines 6–7). Where did Perseus eventually
   find his mother and why was she there?

7 īrātus (line 8).

   (a) What type of word is this?

   (b) Give its comparative and superlative forms.

8 rēgiam (line 8).

   (a) In which case is this word?

   (b) Why is this case used?

9 cucurrit (line 8).

   (a) In which tense is this verb?

   (b) How would you say in Latin **they will run**?

10 effugere (line 9). Which part of the verb is this?

11 frūstrā (line 10). What type of word is this?

12 pessimō (line 10).

   (a) In which case is this word?

   (b) Give the positive and comparative forms of this adjective (nominative
       singular, masculine).

13 ostendit (line 10). What is the connection between this word and the English
   word **ostentatious**?

14 eum (line 11). From which Latin pronoun does this come?

15 posteā … volāvit (lines 12–18). Translate these lines.

Latin	English
Verbs	
eō, īre, iī/īvī, itum	I go
exeō, exīre, exiī, exitum	I go out
ineō, inīre, iniī, initum	I go in
inquit/inquiunt	he/she/they say
nōlī/nōlīte (+ infin.)	do not...
nūntiō, -āre, -āvī, -ātum	I report, announce
occīdō, -ere, occīdī, occīsum	I kill
occupō, -āre, -āvī, -ātum	I seize (a place)
pereō, -īre, -iī, -itum	I die, perish
possum, posse, potuī	I am able
redeō, -īre, -iī, -itum	I go back
redūcō, -ere, redūxī, reductum	I lead back
ruō, -ere, ruī, rutum	I rush
salūtō, -āre, -āvī, -ātum	I greet
trānseō, -īre, -iī, -itum	I go across
Conjuctions	
quamquam	although

The Circus

When the King of Larissa decided to hold some games to entertain his people, and invite people from all over Greece to compete, he was following in a long tradition which has come down to us today in the form of the Olympic Games. The Romans, too, liked these athletic competitions, but for them an even greater spectacle, after the gladiator shows in the amphitheatre, was that of chariot racing in the Circus, most famously the Circus Maximus. This normally involved teams of chariots drawn by four horses (quadrīgae) racing around a track which ran either side of a long central barrier (spīna), at each end of which was a turning point (mēta). The most popular teams were the Russātī (Reds), Venetī (Blues), Albātī (Whites) and Prasinī (Greens), and the charioteers (aurigae) could become very rich. To get an idea of how exciting these chariot races would have been, you might like to watch the famous chariot-racing scene in the film *Ben Hur*.

This topic is part of the Non-Linguistic Studies section of the ISEB syllabus.

■ A Roman mosaic showing a chariot race

Exercise 9.9

(a) (i) Tell the story of how Perseus won the hand of Andromeda in marriage.

   (ii) Do you think it was right for Andromeda's father to give his daughter in marriage to a man she had never met before?

(b) (i) Give an account of a visit to the Circus Maximus in Rome.

   (ii) Which form of entertainment would you have most enjoyed in Rome? Give at least one reason for your answer.

10 Revision and exam practice

Revision: nouns

Exercise 10.1

Give and translate the following forms:

1 Nom. pl. of cīvis
2 Acc. pl. of clāmor
3 Gen. sing. of comes
4 Dat. sing. of coniunx
5 Abl. sing. of corpus
6 Nom. pl. of dōnum
7 Acc. pl. of dux
8 Gen. pl. of flūmen
9 Dat. pl. of frāter
10 Abl. pl. of hostēs

11 Voc. sing. of iuvenis
12 Acc. pl. of līberī
13 Gen. sing. of lūx
14 Dat. pl. of māter
15 Gen. sing. of mīles
16 Abl. pl. of mulier
17 Gen. sing. of nāvis
18 Dat. sing. of nōmen
19 Gen. sing. of pater
20 Abl. sing. of virtūs

Exercise 10.2

Translate into English:

1 arma
2 cōpiārum
3 cum hominibus
4 iter
5 iuvenum
6 in mare
7 ad montem

8 mōram
9 mortem
10 nēmō
11 rēgī
12 senēs
13 sorōrī
14 uxōrēs

15 vōcis
16 vulnera
17 caelum
18 sociōrum
19 virum
20 ventōrum

Revision: adjectives

Exercise 10.3

Give and translate the following forms:

1 Nom. sing. fem. of audāx
2 Acc. pl. masc. of cărus
3 Gen. sing. fem. of crūdēlis
4 Dat. sing. neut. of difficilis
5 Abl. sing. masc. of facilis
6 Nom. pl. fem. of cēterī
7 Acc. pl. neut. of fēlīx
8 Gen. pl. fem. of fortis
9 Dat. pl. masc. of ingēns
10 Abl. sing. neut. of medius
11 Voc. sing. masc. of nōbilis
12 Acc. pl. fem. of mortuus
13 Gen. sing. masc. of omnis
14 Dat. sing. neut. of sapiēns
15 Gen. pl. fem. of paucī
16 Abl. sing. neut. of sōlus
17 Nom. pl. fem. of trīstis
18 Gen. sing. masc. of vīvus
19 Voc. sing. fem. of validus
20 Gen. pl. neut. of nōtus

Exercise 10.4

Translate into English:

1 virī audācis
2 uxor cārissima
3 cēterī servī
4 coniugem suam
5 plūrimōs sociōs
6 magistrī crūdēlis
7 līberī fēlīcēs
8 incolārum fortium
9 flūmina altiora
10 mīlitum mortuōrum
11 equōs parvōs
12 cum omnibus cīvibus
13 poētārum sapientium
14 puerōrum trīstium
15 dea īrātissima
16 servī fessiōrēs
17 ducī saevō
18 poēta pessimus
19 lūx clārissima
20 amīcōs tūtōs

Exercise 10.5

Give and translate the following forms (nom., masc., sing.):

1   Comparative of bonus
2   Superlative of malus
3   Comparative of magnus
4   Superlative of parvus
5   Comparative of multus
6   Superlative of crūdēlis
7   Comparative of facilis
8   Superlative of nōbilis
9   Comparative of malus
10 Superlative of magnus

◯ Revision: pronouns

Exercise 10.6

Translate into English:

1   hic
2   eum
3   illōrum
4   id
5   mihi
6   tibi
7   sibi
8   mēcum
9   illius
10 hōrum
11 haec bella
12 hī cīvēs
13 eius agricolae
14 nōbīs
15 hunc
16 huic
17 eī puellae
18 in eō flūmine
19 vōbīs
20 cum hīs līberīs

◯ Revision: prepositions

Exercise 10.7

Translate into English:

1   ante bellum
2   circum templa
3   contrā hostēs
4   cum ancillīs
5   dē monte
6   ē terrā
7   inter flūmina
8   post proelium
9   per viās
10 prope templum
11 sine sagittīs
12 sub aquā
13 dē virtūte
14 per agrum
15 prope montem
16 super mūrum
17 cum senibus
18 contrā Graecōs
19 prope nāvēs
20 trāns agrōs

Exercise 10.8

Translate into Latin:

1 Towards the leader
2 With the companions
3 On account of the wind
4 Concerning the king
5 Through the streets
6 To the city
7 Down from the sky
8 In the ship
9 Near the old men
10 Because of the wounds

11 In front of the temple
12 Around the town
13 Between the forces
14 Without friends
15 Near the mountains
16 Under the sky
17 Over the wall
18 Across the sea
19 Among the slave-girls
20 After the battles

Revision: verbs

Exercise 10.9

Give and translate the following forms:

1 3rd sing., present of adveniō
2 2nd pl., imperfect of colligō
3 1st pl., perfect of dēbeō
4 Pres. infin. of appropinquō
5 1st sing., pluperfect of errō
6 Pres. infin. of dēfendō
7 Sing. imperative of nārrō
8 1st sing., future of gerō
9 3rd sing., perfect of nūntiō
10 2nd pl., present of occidō

11 3rd pl., imperfect of occupō
12 1st pl., pluperfect of pūniō
13 Sing. imperative of redūcō
14 3rd pl., future of ruō
15 2nd sing., perfect of salūtō
16 1st sing., future of servō
17 Pl. imperative of trādō
18 Pres. infin. of vincō
19 2nd sing., imperfect of vulnerō
20 Pres. infin. of ostendō

Exercise 10.10

Translate into English:

1 spectābunt.
2 colligere.
3 appropinquāverant.
4 dēbētis.
5 errābitis.
6 exspectāverātis.
7 gerētis.

8 inveniunt.
9 liberāte!
10 nārrāvit.
11 occidis.
12 pūnīvit.
13 redūximus.
14 ruunt.

15 salutāveram.
16 servābunt.
17 trādidistī.
18 vīcērunt.
19 vulnerāre.
20 occupāre.

Exercise 10.11

Give and translate the following forms:

1 3rd sing., present of possum
2 2nd pl., imperfect of eō
3 1st pl., perfect of ineō
4 Pres. infin. of exeō
5 2nd sing., future of trānseō
6 Pres. infin. of redeō
7 Sing. imperative of eō
8 1st sing., imperfect of possum
9 3rd sing., perfect of eō
10 2nd pl., future of exeō

11 3rd pl., imperfect of sum
12 1st pl., perfect of possum
13 Sing. imperative of ineō
14 3rd pl., pluperfect of exeō
15 2nd sing., future of pereō
16 1st sing., imperfect of possum
17 Pl. imperative of redeō
18 Pres. infin. of pereō
19 2nd sing., pluperfect of trānseō
20 Pres. infin. of possum

Exercise 10.12

Translate into English:

1 inībant.
2 exīre.
3 potuērunt.
4 redīte.
5 trānsībam.

6 potestis.
7 inierātis.
8 posse.
9 exeunt.
10 exī!

11 cōnspexistī.
12 effūgit.
13 accēpimus.
14 inībunt.
15 redīstī.

16 trānsierant.
17 inīmus.
18 exiērunt.
19 redītis.
20 trānsīre.

Revision: questions

Exercise 10.13

Translate into English:

1 nōnne urbem capere cupit?

2 num fēminās īratās spectābis?

3 cūr ancillae trīstēs exiērunt?

4 nōnne, virī, ad oppidum appropinquātis?

5 senēsne rēgīnam spectant?

6 parābisne cibum meliōrem?

7 num in proeliō pugnāre poterant?

8 ubi erant amīcī optimī?

9 inītisne in urbem magnam?

10 cūr vīnum nōn biberās?

Revision: concessive clauses and prohibitions

Exercise 10.14

1 dux, quamquam urbem capere cupiēbat, rediit.

2 fēminās spectābis, quamquam eās timēs.

3 ancillae, quamquam fessae erant, exiērunt.

4 agricolae, quamquam ad oppidum appropinquābant, trīstēs erant.

5 cīvis, quamquam uxōrem amābat, eam occīdit.

6 nōlī cibum equō meō dare!

7 nōlīte in agrum festīnāre!

8 nōlī ex templō exīre!

9 nōlīte flūmen altum trānsīre!

10 nōlī ad īnsulam parvam nāvigāre!

Revision: adverbs, conjunctions, etc.

Exercise 10.15

Translate into English:

1 antequam	6 herī	11 quoque	16 iterum
2 celeriter	7 nam	12 tum	17 deinde
3 crās	8 nunc	13 itaque	18 tamen
4 forte	9 posteā	14 statim	19 tandem
5 frūstrā	10 quamquam	15 mox	20 numquam

Revision: numerals

Exercise 10.16

Translate into English:

1 ūndecim	8 duodēvīgintī	15 quārtus
2 quattuor	9 quīndecim	16 duodecim
3 tredecim	10 sēdecim	17 ūndēvīgintī
4 septem	11 vīgintī	18 trēs
5 nōnus	12 septendecim	19 quīntus
6 septimus	13 sextus	20 quattuordecim
7 octāvus	14 quīnque	

Exercise 10.17

Translate into Latin:

1 Seventeen	6 Sixth
2 Fifteen	7 Twenty
3 Second	8 Fourth
4 Fifth	9 Eleven
5 Nineteen	10 Thirteen

◯ Revision: translating into Latin

Exercise 10.18

Translate into Latin:

1 The friends loved good wine.

2 The queen sees the big arrows.

3 The boys have tired horses.

4 We did not fear the danger.

5 The savage master was warning the slaves.

6 The girl was calling the messengers.

7 She loved the small gifts.

8 The poet saw the money.

9 The sailors feared large winds.

10 The inhabitants watched the tired slave-girls.

◯ Exam practice

The next exercise provides practice in the format of the Level 2 Common Entrance exam. Marks are given in brackets.

Exercise 10.19

1 Study the following passage and answer the questions below:

The death of Eurydice

Orpheus, deī Apollinis fīlius, in Thraciā habitābat. ubi cantābat, omnēs hominēs, etiam flūmina et montēs, eum audīre cupiēbant. uxor eius, nōmine Eurydicē, nympha pulcherrima erat. hanc Orpheus magnopere amāvit et diū laetissimī erant.

5 ōlim tamen Eurydicē cum amīcīs in silvīs ambulābat. subitō serpēns ad eam appropinquāvit. nympham momordit et vulnerāvit. mox Eurydicē periit et Orpheus trīstissimus erat.

nympha, -ae, f. nymph
silva, -ae, f. wood
serpēns, serpentis, f. snake
mordeō, -ere, momordī I bite

(a) ubi cantābat, omnēs hominēs, etiam flūmina et montēs, eum audīre cupiēbant (lines 1–2).

What happened when Orpheus began to sing? (4)

(b) uxor eius, nōmine Eurydicē, nympha pulcherrima erat (lines 2–3).

Who was Eurydice? (2)

(c) hanc Orpheus magnopere amāvit et diū laetissimī erant (lines 3–4).

What do we learn about Orpheus and Eurydice in these lines? (2)

(d) ōlim tamen Eurydicē cum amīcīs in silvīs ambulābat (line 5).

Translate the Latin words that tell us who was with Eurydice in the woods. (2)

(e) subitō serpēns ad eam appropinquāvit (lines 5–6).

What do we learn about the snake in these lines? (1)

(f) nympham momordit et vulnerāvit (line 6).

What did the snake do to Eurydice? (2)

(g) mox Eurydicē periit et Orpheus miserrimus erat (lines 6–7).

What happened at the end of the story? (2)

(15 marks)

2 Translate the following passage into good English, writing your translation on alternate lines.

Orpheus ventures into the Underworld

Orpheus uxōris clāmōrēs audīvit et in <u>silvās</u> statim iniit; <u>nec tamen</u> fēminam miseram servāre potuit. Orpheus, quod eam diū amāverat, trīstissimus erat. tandem ad <u>Tartarum</u>, quod uxōrem cāram invenīre cupīvit, festīnāvit.

5   mox ad <u>Tartarum</u> iuvenis fortis advēnit et ad <u>Plūtōnem</u>, rēgem <u>Tartarī</u>, appropinquāvit. 'ad terram <u>mortālium</u> coniugem meam redūcere cupiō,' inquit. 'fēmina misera tēcum habitāre nōn cupit. nōnne auxilium nōbīs dabis?'

> silva, -ae, f. = wood
> nec tamen = but … not
> Tartarus, -ī, m. = the Underworld
> Plūtō, -ōnis, m. = Pluto
> mortālēs, -ium, m. pl. = mortals

(30 marks)

3 Study the following passage and answer the questions below.

> Plūtō, ubi hoc audīvit, iuvenī fortī haec respondit: 'tuam uxōrem,' inquit,
> 'ad terram mortālium redūc. nōlī tamen eam respicere! sī id faciēs,
> numquam eam vīvam iterum vidēbis.' Orpheus tamen, ubi ad terram
> mortālium paene advēnit, respexit et Eurydice statim ad Tartarum rediit.
> 5 tum Orpheus per terrās miserrimus errābat et carmina trīstissima
> cantābat. tandem mulierēs saevae eum occīdērunt. caput eius abscīdērunt et
> in flūmen Hebrum iēcērunt. iuvenis tamen, quamquam mortuus erat,
> carmina trīstia post mortem suam semper cantābat.

> mortālēs, -ium, m. pl. = mortals
> respiciō, -ere, respexī = I look back
> paene = almost
> Tartarus, -ī, m. = the Underworld
> carmen, -inis, n. = song
> abscīdō, -ere, abscīdī = I cut off
> Hebrus, -ī, m. = Hebrus (a river in Thrace)

(a) hoc (line 1). In which case is this word?   (1)

(b) fortī (line 1). Give the comparative and superlative forms of this
     adjective, keeping the case and gender the same.   (2)

(c) eam (line 2). What type of pronoun is this?   (1)

(d) vidēbis (line 3). Put this verb into the present tense, keeping the
     person and number the same.   (1)

(e) tamen (line 3). What type of word is this?   (1)

(f) terrās (line 5). In which case is this word? Why is this case used?   (2)

(g) iēcērunt (line 7). In which tense is this verb? Give the first person
     singular, present tense of this verb.   (2)

(h) mortuus (line 7). What is the connection between this word and the
     English word **mortuary**?   (2)

(i) Translate the following sentences into Latin, using the vocabulary
     given below.

     (i)   The bad queen was hurrying into the temple.   (4)

     (ii) The inhabitants see the tired slaves.   (4)

     bad = malus, -a, -um   inhabitant = incola, -ae, c.

     queen = regina, -ae, f.   I see = video (2)

     I hurry = festino (1)   tired = fessus, -a, -um

     into = in + acc.   slave = servus, -i, m.

     temple = templum, -i, n.

                                              (20 marks)

4 Answer any *one* of the following eight questions (a–h). Make sure you answer both parts (i) and (ii).

Domestic life

(a) (i) You have been invited to a Roman dinner party. Explain some of the different courses of food, and some of the entertainment, which you might expect to receive during the evening. (8)

(ii) Which kinds of Roman food would you *not* like to have sampled? Explain your answers. (2)

(b) (i) You are getting ready to go out to the forum with your family. Describe what you and the other members of your family are wearing. (8)

(ii) How different are the clothes you have described above from the ones you wear today? Give two examples. (2)

The city of Rome

(c) (i) Tell the story of Horatius. (8)

(ii) Which elements of this story would the Romans have found particularly admirable? Explain your answer. (2)

(d) (i) Describe a typical day at the Circus Maximus. (8)

(ii) Which form of entertainment in today's world does this most remind you of? Explain your answer. (2)

The army and Roman Britain

(e) (i) Describe and give the Latin terms for the most important kinds of equipment and weaponry which a Roman soldier would carry with him. (8)

(ii) Name two items of a Roman soldier's equipment and weaponry that a soldier today might still find useful. Explain your choices. (2)

(f) (i) Give an account of Julius Caesar's two invasions of Britain. (8)

(ii) Would it be accurate to say that Julius Caesar conquered Britain? Explain your answer. (2)

Greek mythology

(g) (i) Give an account of the causes and main events of the Trojan War. (8)

(ii) Why do you think the story of the Trojan War proved so popular to the Ancient Greeks? (2)

(h) (i) Tell the story of Odysseus's encounter with Circe. (8)

(ii) What would you consider to have been Odysseus's main qualities in this or any other of his adventures? Explain your answer. (2)

(Total marks: 75, to be expressed as a percentage)

Guide to pronunciation

Vowels

The main problem with learning to pronounce Latin correctly is the vowels. The Romans pronounced their vowels as follows:

ă (short)	as in cup	ā (long)	as in calf
ĕ (short)	as in set	ē (long)	as in stair
ĭ (short)	as in bit	ī (long)	as in bee
ŏ (short)	as in lot	ō (long)	as in the French *beau*
ŭ (short)	as in put	ū (long)	as in route

The one that looks most odd here is the short ă. It really was pronounced like the u in cup, not the a in hat.

In this book, *long* vowels are marked with a macron (ā, ē, ī, ō, ū). If they are *not* marked, they are short. Occasionally a short vowel is *marked* as short (ă, ĕ, ĭ, ŏ, ŭ) if there is an incorrect tendency to pronounce the vowel long. For example the o in the Latin words egŏ and duŏ are marked as short because so many people pronounce the words as if they were long.

A vowel is regularly pronounced long when followed by ns or nf. This rule even applies across a word junction, so for example to the word in when this is followed by a word starting with s or f.

E.g. **in** agrō but **in** suō agrō.

A few words, such as ibi, ubi and octo, end in vowels which can be pronounced long or short. In these cases, we have not marked the vowel, but in practice you will probably find it easier to pronounce the vowel as long.

Diphthongs

Where two vowels are pronounced as *one* sound (as in the English *boil*, or *wait*), this is called a **diphthong** and the resulting syllable will always be long. For example the -ae at the end of the word puellae is a diphthong. Diphthongs, because they are always long, are not marked with a macron.

The most common diphthongs are:

ae   as in eye
au   as in now

Both of these diphthongs are found in the Latin word nautae = sailors.

Where two vowels come together but are NOT a diphthong, the first vowel will always be pronounced short. Thus, the **ue** in the word p**ue**llae is not a diphthong (the word has three syllables), and the u is thus pronounced short: **pŭ-ell-ae**.

Consonants

- C is always 'hard' as in cot, never 'soft' as in century.
- R is always rolled.
- S is always 's' as in bus, never 'z' as in busy.
- V is pronounced as a W.
- GN is pronounced NGN, as in hangnail.
- Latin has no letter J. The Romans used i as a consonant instead (thus Iūlius Caesar, pronounced Yulius).
- M, at the end of a word, was nasalised and reduced (i.e. only partially pronounced).

Stress

Just as in English we have a particular way of stressing words, so they did in Latin. We, for example, say potáto (with the stress on the a). When we learn English words, we automatically learn how to stress them. This would have been the same for the Romans, learning Latin words.

The Romans worked out how to stress a word by looking at its penultimate syllable. Syllables are either long or short. They are long if they contain a long vowel, or if they contain a short vowel followed by two consonants. They are short if they contain a short vowel which is *not* followed by two consonants. Using this information, a Latin word should be stressed as follows:

- The final syllable of a word should never be stressed (e.g. ámō, ámās, ámat, etc.)
- In a word of more than two syllables, if the penultimate syllable is long, stress it (e.g. amātis is stressed amátis; amāvistis is stressed amāvístis).
- If the penultimate syllable is short, stress the the one before it (e.g. regĭtis is stressed régitis).

Summary of grammar

◯ Regular verbs

Present infinitive: *To love*

amāre	monēre	regere	audīre	capere

Present: *I love, I am loving, I do love*

amō	moneō	regō	audiō	capiō
amās	monēs	regis	audīs	capis
amat	monet	regit	audit	capit
amāmus	monēmus	regimus	audīmus	capimus
amātis	monētis	regitis	audītis	capitis
amant	monent	regunt	audiunt	capiunt

Future: *I shall love*

amābō	monēbō	regam	audiam	capiam
amābis	monēbis	regēs	audiēs	capiēs
amābit	monēbit	reget	audiet	capiet
amābimus	monēbimus	regēmus	audiēmus	capiēmus
amābitis	monēbitis	regētis	audiētis	capiētis
amābunt	monēbunt	regent	audient	capient

Imperfect: *I was loving, I loved, I used to love*

amābam	monēbam	regēbam	audiēbam	capiēbam
amābās	monēbās	regēbās	audiēbās	capiēbās
amābat	monēbat	regēbat	audiēbat	capiēbat
amābāmus	monēbāmus	regēbāmus	audiēbāmus	capiēbāmus
amābātis	monēbātis	regēbātis	audiēbātis	capiēbātis
amābant	monēbant	regēbant	audiēbant	capiēbant

Perfect: *I have loved, I loved*

amāvī	monuī	rēxī	audīvī	cēpī
amāvistī	monuistī	rēxistī	audīvistī	cēpistī
amāvit	monuit	rēxit	audīvit	cēpit
amāvimus	monuimus	rēximus	audīvimus	cēpimus
amāvistis	monuistis	rēxistis	audīvistis	cēpistis
amāvērunt	monuērunt	rēxērunt	audīvērunt	cēpērunt

Pluperfect: *I had loved*

amāveram	monueram	rēxeram	audīveram	cēperam
amāverās	monuerās	rēxerās	audīverās	cēperās
amāverat	monuerat	rēxerat	audīverat	cēperat
amāverāmus	monuerāmus	rēxerāmus	audīverāmus	cēperāmus
amāverātis	monuerātis	rēxerātis	audīverātis	cēperātis
amāverant	monuerant	rēxerant	audīverant	cēperant

Imperatives: *Love!*

amā	monē	regĕ	audī	capĕ
amāte	monēte	regĭte	audīte	capĭte

Irregular verbs: sum = *I am*; possum = *I am able*; eō = *I go*

Present infinitive

esse   posse   īre

Present

sum	possum	eō
es	potes	īs
est	potest	it
sumus	possumus	īmus
estis	potestis	ītis
sunt	possunt	eunt

Future

erō	poterō	ibō
eris	poteris	ibis
erit	poterit	ibit
erimus	poterimus	ibimus
eritis	poteritis	ibitis
erunt	poterunt	ibunt

Imperfect

eram	poteram	ibam
erās	poterās	ibās
erat	poterat	ibat
erāmus	poterāmus	ibāmus
erātis	poterātis	ibātis
erant	poterant	ibant

Perfect

fuī	potuī	iī
fuistī	potuistī	īstī
fuit	potuit	iit
fuimus	potuimus	iimus
fuistis	potuistis	īstis
fuērunt	potuērunt	iērunt

Imperatives

es	–	ī
este	–	īte

◯ Nouns

1st declension

Nominative	puella
Vocative	puella
Accusative	puellam
Genitive	puellae
Dative	puellae
Ablative	puellā
Nominative	puellae
Vocative	puellae
Accusative	puellās
Genitive	puellārum
Dative	puellīs
Ablative	puellīs

2nd declension

Nominative	dominus	puer	magister	bellum
Vocative	domine	puer	magister	bellum
Accusative	dominum	puerum	magistrum	bellum
Genitive	dominī	puerī	magistrī	bellī
Dative	dominō	puerō	magistrō	bellō
Ablative	dominō	puerō	magistrō	bellō
Nominative	dominī	puerī	magistrī	bella
Vocative	dominī	puerī	magistrī	bella
Accusative	dominōs	puerōs	magistrōs	bella
Genitive	dominōrum	puerōrum	magistrōrum	bellōrum
Dative	dominīs	puerīs	magistrīs	bellīs
Ablative	dominīs	puerīs	magistrīs	bellīs

2nd declension irregular

Nominative	fīlius	deus	vir
Vocative	fīlī	deus	vir
Accusative	fīlium	deum	virum
Genitive	fīliī (fīlī)	deī	virī
Dative	fīliō	deō	virō
Ablative	fīliō	deō	virō
Nominative	fīliī	dī (deī)	virī
Vocative	fīliī	dī (deī)	virī
Accusative	fīliōs	deōs	virōs
Genitive	fīliōrum	deōrum (deum)	virōrum (virum)
Dative	fīliīs	dīs (deīs)	virīs
Ablative	fīliīs	dīs (deīs)	virīs

3rd declension: increasing

	M/F	N
Nominative	rēx	corpus
Vocative	rēx	corpus
Accusative	rēgem	corpus
Genitive	rēgis	corporis
Dative	rēgī	corporī
Ablative	rēge	corpore
Nominative	rēgēs	corpora
Vocative	rēgēs	corpora
Accusative	rēgēs	corpora
Genitive	rēgum	corporum
Dative	rēgibus	corporibus
Ablative	rēgibus	corporibus

3rd declension: non-increasing

Nominative	cīvis	mare
Vocative	cīvis	mare
Accusative	cīvem	mare
Genitive	cīvis	maris
Dative	cīvī	marī
Ablative	cīve	marī
Nominative	cīvēs	maria
Vocative	cīvēs	maria
Accusative	cīvēs	maria
Genitive	cīvium	marium
Dative	cīvibus	maribus
Ablative	cīvibus	maribus

◯ Adjectives

1st/2nd declension in -us

	M	F	N
Nominative	bonus	bona	bonum
Vocative	bone	bona	bonum
Accusative	bonum	bonam	bonum
Genitive	bonī	bonae	bonī
Dative	bonō	bonae	bonō
Ablative	bonō	bonā	bonō
Nominative	bonī	bonae	bona
Vocative	bonī	bonae	bona
Accusative	bonōs	bonās	bona
Genitive	bonōrum	bonārum	bonōrum
Dative	bonīs	bonīs	bonīs
Ablative	bonīs	bonīs	bonīs

1st/2nd declension in -er

	M	F	N
Nominative	miser	misera	miserum
Vocative	miser	misera	miserum
Accusative	miserum	miseram	miserum
Genitive	miserī	miserae	miserī
Dative	miserō	miserae	miserō
Ablative	miserō	miserā	miserō
Nominative	miserī	miserae	misera
Vocative	miserī	miserae	misera
Accusative	miserōs	miserās	misera
Genitive	miserōrum	miserārum	miserōrum
Dative	miserīs	miserīs	miserīs
Ablative	miserīs	miserīs	miserīs
Nominative	pulcher	pulchra	pulchrum
Vocative	pulcher	pulchra	pulchrum
Accusative	pulchrum	pulchram	pulchrum
Genitive	pulchrī	pulchrae	pulchrī
Dative	pulchrō	pulchrae	pulchrō
Ablative	pulchrō	pulchrā	pulchrō
Nominative	pulchrī	pulchrae	pulchra
Vocative	pulchrī	pulchrae	pulchra
Accusative	pulchrōs	pulchrās	pulchra
Genitive	pulchrōrum	pulchrārum	pulchrōrum
Dative	pulchrīs	pulchrīs	pulchrīs
Ablative	pulchrīs	pulchrīs	pulchrīs

3rd declension: one termination

	M	F	N
Nominative	ingēns	ingēns	ingēns
Vocative	ingēns	ingēns	ingēns
Accusative	ingentem	ingentem	ingēns
Genitive	ingentis	ingentis	ingentis
Dative	ingentī	ingentī	ingentī
Ablative	ingentī	ingentī	ingentī
Nominative	ingentēs	ingentēs	ingentia
Vocative	ingentēs	ingentēs	ingentia
Accusative	ingentēs	ingentēs	ingentia
Genitive	ingentium	ingentium	ingentium
Dative	ingentibus	ingentibus	ingentibus
Ablative	ingentibus	ingentibus	ingentibus

3rd declension: two termination

	M	F	N
Nominative	trīstis	trīstis	trīste
Vocative	trīstis	trīstis	trīste
Accusative	trīstem	trīstem	trīste
Genitive	trīstis	trīstis	trīstis
Dative	trīstī	trīstī	trīstī
Ablative	trīstī	trīstī	trīstī
Nominative	trīstēs	trīstēs	trīstia
Vocative	trīstēs	trīstēs	trīstia
Accusative	trīstēs	trīstēs	trīstia
Genitive	trīstium	trīstium	trīstium
Dative	trīstibus	trīstibus	trīstibus
Ablative	trīstibus	trīstibus	trīstibus

Comparative adjectives

	M	F	N
Nominative	melior	melior	melius
Vocative	melior	melior	melius
Accusative	meliōrem	meliōrem	melius
Genitive	meliōris	meliōris	meliōris
Dative	meliōrī	meliōrī	meliōrī
Ablative	meliōre	meliōre	meliōre
Nominative	meliōrēs	meliōrēs	meliōra
Vocative	meliōrēs	meliōrēs	meliōra
Accusative	meliōrēs	meliōrēs	meliōra
Genitive	meliōrum	meliōrum	meliōrum
Dative	meliōribus	meliōribus	meliōribus
Ablative	meliōribus	meliōribus	meliōribus

Personal and reflexive pronouns

Nominative	egŏ	tū	nōs	vōs	–
Accusative	mē	tē	nōs	vōs	sē
Genitive	mei	tui	nostrum	vestrum	suī
Dative	mihi	tibi	nobis	vobis	sibi
Ablative	me	te	nobis	vobis	sē

Demonstrative pronouns

is, ea, id = that (he, she, it)

	M	F	N
Nominative	is	ea	id
Vocative	–	–	–
Accusative	eum	eam	id
Genitive	eius	eius	eius
Dative	eī	eī	eī
Ablative	eō	eā	eō
Nominative	eī	eae	ea
Vocative	–	–	–
Accusative	eōs	eās	ea
Genitive	eōrum	eārum	eōrum
Dative	eīs	eīs	eīs
Ablative	eīs	eīs	eīs

hic, haec, hoc = *this* (near me) [plural = *these*]

Nominative	hic	haec	hoc
Accusative	hunc	hanc	hoc
Genitive	huius	huius	huius
Dative	huic	huic	huic
Ablative	hōc	hāc	hōc
Nominative	hī	hae	haec
Accusative	hōs	hās	haec
Genitive	hōrum	hārum	hōrum
Dative	hīs	hīs	hīs
Ablative	hīs	hīs	hīs

ille, illa, illud = *that* (over there) [plural = *those*]

	M	F	N
Nominative	ille	illa	illud
Accusative	illum	illam	illud
Genitive	illius	illius	illius
Dative	illī	illī	illī
Ablative	illō	illā	illō
Nominative	illī	illae	illa
Accusative	illōs	illās	illa
Genitive	illōrum	illārum	illōrum
Dative	illīs	illīs	illīs
Ablative	illīs	illīs	illīs

Cardinal numerals

1	I	ūnus	11	XI	ūndecim
2	II	duŏ	12	XII	duodecim
3	III	trēs	13	XIII	tredecim
4	IV/IIII	quattuor	14	XIV	quattuordecim
5	V	quīnque	15	XV	quīndecim
6	VI	sex	16	XVI	sēdecim
7	VII	septem	17	XVII	septendecim
8	VIII	octo	18	XVIII	duodēvīgintī
9	IX	novem	19	XIX	ūndēvīgintī
10	X	decem	20	XX	vīgintī

◯ Ordinals

1st	prīmus	6th	sextus
2nd	secundus	7th	septimus
3rd	tertius	8th	octāvus
4th	quārtus	9th	nōnus
5th	quīntus	10th	decimus

Latin – English vocabulary

ā/ab + abl. = by, from
absum, abesse, āfuī = I am absent
accipiō, -ere, accēpī, acceptum = I receive
ad + acc. = to, towards
adsum, adesse, adfuī = I am present
adveniō, -īre, advēnī, adventum = I arrive
aedificō, -āre, -āvī, -ātum = I build
ager, agrī, m. = field
agricola, -ae, m. = farmer
altus, -a, -um = high, deep
amīcus, amīcī, m. = friend
amō, -āre, -āvī, -ātum = I love, like
ancilla, -ae, f. = slave-girl
ante + acc. = before
antequam = before
appropinquō, -āre, -āvī, -ātum = I approach
aqua, -ae, f. = water
arma, -ōrum, n. pl. = weapons, arms
audāx, audācis = bold
audiō, audīre, audīvī, audītum = I hear
aurum, -ī, n. = gold
autem = however, moreover
auxilium, -iī, n. = help
bellum, bellī, n. = war
bene = well
bibō, bibere, bibī = I drink
bonus, -a, -um = good
caelum, -ī, n. = sky
cantō, -āre, -āvī, -ātum = I sing
capiō, -ere, cēpī, captum = I capture, take
cārus, -a, -um = dear
celeriter = quickly
cēterī, -ae, -a = the rest, others
cibus, cibī, m. = food
circum + acc. = around
cīvis, cīvis, c. = citizen
clāmō, -āre, -āvī, -ātum = I shout
clāmor, clāmōris, m. = shout
clārus, -a, -um = famous, clear, bright
colligō, -ere, collēgī, collēctum = I collect
comes, comitis, c. = companion
coniūnx, coniugis, c. = husband, wife
cōnspiciō, -ere, cōnspexī, cōnspectum = I catch
    sight of
cōnstituō, -ere, cōnstituī, cōnstitūtum = I decide
cōnsūmō, -ere, cōnsūmpsī, cōnsūmptum = I eat

contrā + acc. = against
cōpiae, -ārum, f. pl. = forces
corpus, corporis, n. = body
crās = tomorrow
crūdēlis, -e = cruel
cum + abl. = with
cupiō, -ere, cupīvī, cupītum = I want, desire
cūr? = why?
currō, currere, cucurrī, cursum = I run
dē + abl. = down from, concerning
dea, -ae, f. = goddess
dēbeō, -ēre, dēbuī, dēbitum = I owe, ought
decem = ten
decimus, -a, -um = tenth
dēfendō, -ere, dēfendī, dēfēnsum = I defend
deinde = then
dēleō, -ēre, dēlēvī, dēlētum = I destroy
deus, deī, m. = god
dīcō, dīcere, dīxī, dictum = I say
difficilis, -e = difficult
discēdō, -ere, discessī, discessum = I depart
diū = for a long time
dō, dăre, dedī, dătum = I give
dominus, dominī, m. = lord, master
dōnum, -ī, n. = gift
dormiō, -īre, -īvī, -ītum = I sleep
dūcō, dūcere, dūxī, ductum = I lead
duŏ = two
duodecim = twelve
duodēvīgintī = eighteen
dux, ducis, m. = leader
ē/ex + abl. = out of
effugiō, -ere, effūgī = I escape
egŏ = I
eō, īre, iī/īvī, itum = I go
equus, equī, m. = horse
errō, -āre, -āvī, -ātum = I wander
et ... et = both ... and
et = and
etiam = also, even
exeō, exīre, exiī, exitum = I go out
exspectō, -āre, -āvī, -ātum = I wait for
facilis, -e = easy
faciō, -ere, fēcī, factum = I do, make
fēlīx, fēlīcis = fortunate
fēmina, -ae, f. = woman

fessus, -a, -um = tired
festīnō, -āre, -āvī, -ātum = I hurry
fīlia, -ae, f. = daughter
fīlius, fīliī, m. = son
flūmen, flūminis, n. = river
forte = by chance
fortis, -e = brave, strong
fortiter = bravely
frāter, frātris, m. = brother
frūstrā = in vain
fugiō, -ere, fūgī, fugitum = I flee
gerō, -ere, gessī, gestum = I carry on, wear
gladius, gladiī, m. = sword
Graecus, -a, -um = Greek
habeō, -ēre, habuī, habitum = I have
habitō, -āre, -āvī, -ātum = I live (in)
hasta, -ae, f. = spear
herī = yesterday
hīc = here
hic, haec, hoc = this
homō, hominis, m. = man, woman
hostis, hostis, c. = enemy
iaciō, -ere, iēcī, iactum = I throw
iam = now, already
ibi = there
igitur = therefore
ille, illa, illud = that
in + abl. = in, on
in + acc. = into, on to
incola, -ae, c. = inhabitant
ineō, inīre, iniī, initum = I go in
ingēns, ingentis = huge
inquit/inquiunt = he/she/they say
īnsula, -ae, f. = island
inter + acc. = between, among
intrō, -āre, -āvī, -ātum = I enter
inveniō, -īre, invēnī, inventum = I find
īra, -ae, f. = anger
īrātus, -a, -um = angry
is, ea, id = that
itaque = therefore
iter, itineris, n. = journey
iterum = again
iubeō, -ēre, iussī, iussum = I order
iuvenis, iuvenis, c. = young man, young person
labōrō, -āre, -āvī, -ātum = I work
laetus, -a, -um = happy
laudō, -āre, -āvī, -ātum = I praise
legō, legere, lēgī, lectum = I read, choose

liber, librī, m. = book
līberī, -ōrum, m. pl. = children
līberō, -āre, -āvī, -ātum = I free
locus, -ī, m. = place
longus, -a, -um = long
lūdō, -ere, lūsī, lūsum = I play
lūx, lūcis, f. = light
magister, magistrī, m. = master
magnopere = greatly, very much
magnus, -a, -um = big, great
malus, -a, -um = bad
maneō, -ēre, mānsī, mānsum = I remain
mare, maris, n. = sea
māter, mātris, f. = mother
medius, -a, -um = middle
mīles, mīlitis, m. = soldier
miser, misera, miserum = miserable, wretched,
    unhappy
mittō, mittere, mīsī, missum = I send
moneō, -ēre, monuī, monitum = I warn, advise
mōns, montis, m. = mountain
mōra, -ae, f. = delay
mors, mortis, f. = death
mortuus, -a, -um = dead
moveō, -ēre, mōvī, mōtum = I move
mox = soon
mulier, mulieris, f. = woman
multus, -a, -um = much, many
mūrus, mūrī, m. = wall
nam = for
nārrō, -āre, -āvī, -ātum = I tell
nauta, -ae, m. = sailor
nāvigō, -āre, -āvī, -ātum = I sail
nāvis, nāvis, f. = ship
-ne...? asks a question
necō, -āre, -āvī, -ātum = I kill
nēmō, nūllius, c. = no one
nihil = nothing
nōbilis, -e = noble
nōlī/nōlīte (+ infin.) = do not...
nōmen, nōminis, n. = name
nōn = not
nōnne? introduces a question expecting the answer
    'yes'
nōnus, -a, -um = ninth
nōs = we
noster, nostra, nostrum = our
nōtus, -a, -um = well-known
novem = nine

novus, -a, -um = new

num? introduces a question expecting the answer 'no'

numquam = never

nunc = now

nūntiō, -āre, -āvī, -ātum = I report, announce

nūntius, nūntiī, m. = messenger,

occīdō, -ere, occīdī, occīsum = I kill

occupō, -āre, -āvī, -ātum = I seize (a place)

octāvus, -a, -um = eighth

octo = eight

ōlim = once upon a time

omnis, -e = all, every

oppidum, oppidī, n. = town

oppugnō, -āre, -āvī, -ātum = I attack

ostendō, -ere, ostendī, ostentum = I show

parēns, parentis, c. = parent

parō, -āre, -āvī, -ātum = I prepare

pars, partis, f. = part

parvus, -a, -um = small

pater, patris, m. = father

patria, -ae, f. = country, fatherland

paucī, -ae, -a = few

per + acc. = through

pereō, -īre, -iī, -itum = I die, perish

perīculum, perīculī, n. = danger

perterritus, -a, -um = terrified

poēta, -ae, m. = poet

pōnō, -ere, posuī, positum = I place

portō, -āre, -āvī, -ātum = I carry

possum, posse, potuī = I am able

post + acc. = after

posteā = afterwards

postquam = after

prīmus, -a, -um = first

prō + abl. = on behalf of, in place of, in front of

proelium, -iī, n. = battle

prope + acc. = near

propter + acc. = on account of

puella, -ae, f. = girl

puer, puerī, m. = boy

pugnō, -āre, -āvī, -ātum = I fight

pulcher, pulchra, pulchrum = beautiful

pūniō, -īre, pūnīvī, pūnītum = I punish

quam = how

quamquam = although

quārtus, -a, -um = fourth

quattuor = four

quattuordecim = fourteen

-que = and

quid? = what?

quīndecim = fifteen

quīnque = five

quīntus, -a, -um = fifth

quis? = who?

quod = because

quoque = also

redeō, -īre, -iī, -itum = I go back

redūcō, -ere, redūxī, reductum = I lead back

rēgīna, -ae, f. = queen

regō, regere, rēxī, rēctum = I rule

respondeō, -ēre, respondī, respōnsum = I answer

rēx, rēgis, m. = king

rīdeō, -ēre, rīsī, rīsum = I hold

rogō, -āre, -āvī, -ātum = I ask

Rōmānus, -a, -um = Roman

ruō, -ere, ruī, rutum = I rush

sacer, sacra, sacrum = sacred

saepe = often

saevus, -a, -um = savage

sagitta, -ae, f. = arrow

salūtō, -āre, -āvī, -ātum = I greet

sapiēns, sapientis = wise

scrībō, -ere, scrīpsī, scriptum = I write

scūtum, scūtī, n. = shield

sē = himself, herself, itself, themselves (reflexive)

secundus, -a, -um = second

sed = but

sēdecim = sixteen

semper = always

senex, senis, m. = old man

septem = seven

septendecim = seventeen

septimus, -a, -um = seventh

servō, -āre, -āvī, -ātum = I save

servus, servī, m. = slave

sex = six

sextus, -a, -um = sixth

sīc = so, thus

sine + abl. = without

socius, -iī, m. = companion, ally

sōlus, -a, -um = alone

soror, sorōris, f. = sister

spectō, -āre, -āvī, -ātum = I watch

statim = immediately

stō, -āre, stetī, stătum = I stand

sub + abl. = under

subitō = suddenly

sum, esse, fuī = I am

super + acc. = over

superō, -āre, -āvī, -ātum = I overcome

suus, -a, -um = his own, her own, its own, their own

tamen = however

tandem = at last

templum, templī, n. = temple

teneō, -ēre, tenuī, tentum = I hold

terra, -ae, f. = land, ground

terreō, -ēre, terruī, territum = I frighten

tertius, -a, -um = third

timeō, -ēre, timuī = I fear

trādō, -ere, trādidī, trāditum = I hand over

trāns + acc. = across

trānseō, -īre, -iī, -itum = I go across

tredecim = thirteen

trēs = three

trīstis, -e = sad

tū = you (sing.)

tum = then

turba, -ae, f. = crowd

tūtus, -a, -um = safe

tuus, -a, -um = your (of you (sing.))

ubi = when

ubi? = where?

unda, -ae, f. = wave

ūndecim = eleven

ūndēvīgintī = nineteen

ūnus = one

urbs, urbis, f. = city

uxor, uxōris, f. = wife

validus, -a, -um = strong

veniō, venīre, vēnī, ventum = I come

ventus, -ī, m. = wind

verbum, verbī, n. = word

vester, vestra, vestrum = your (of you (pl.))

via, -ae, f. = road, street, way

videō, -ēre, vīdī, vīsum = I see

vīgintī = twenty

vincō, -ere, vīcī, victum = I conquer

vīnum, -ī, n. = wine

vir, virī, m. = man

virtūs, virtūtis, f. = courage

vīvus, -a, -um = alive

vocō, -āre, -āvī, -ātum = I call

vōs = you (pl.)

vōx, vōcis, f. = voice

vulnerō, -āre, -āvī, -ātum = I wound

vulnus, vulneris, n. = wound

English–Latin vocabulary

Able, I am = possum, posse, potuī
About (concerning) = dē + abl.
Absent, I am = absum, abesse, āfuī
Across = trāns + acc.
Advise, I = moneō, -ēre, monuī, monitum
After (preposition) = post + acc.
After (conjunction) = postquam
Afterwards = posteā
Again = iterum
Against = contrā + acc.
Alive = vīvus, -a, -um
All = omnis, -e
Alone = sōlus, -a, -um
Along = per + acc.
Already = iam
Also = etiam
Also = quoque
Although = quamquam
Always = semper
Am, I = sum, esse, fuī
Among = inter + acc.
And = et; -que
Anger = īra, -ae, f.
Angry = īrātus, -a, -um
Announce, I = nūntiō, -āre, -āvī, -ātum
Answer, I = respondeō, -ēre, respondī, respōnsum
Approach, I = appropinquō, -āre, -āvī, -ātum
    (+ ad or + dative)
Arms = arma, -ōrum, n. pl.
Around = circum + acc.
Arrive, I = adveniō, -īre, advēnī, adventum
Arrow = sagitta, -ae, f.
Ask, I = rogō, -āre, -āvī, -ātum
At last = tandem
Attack, I = oppugnō, -āre, -āvī, -ātum
Bad = malus, -a, -um
Battle = proelium, -iī, n.
Beautiful = pulcher, pulchra, pulchrum
Because = quod
Because of = propter + acc.
Before (preposition) = ante + acc.
Before (conjunction) = antequam
Between = inter + acc.
Big = magnus, -a, -um
Body = corpus, corporis, n.
Bold = audāx, audācis

Book = liber, librī, m.
Both … and = et … et
Boy = puer, puerī, m.
Brave = fortis, -e
Bravely = fortiter
Bright = clārus, -a, -um
Brother = frāter, frātris, m.
Build, I = aedificō, -āre, -āvī, -ātum
But = sed
By chance = forte
Call, I = vocō, -āre, -āvī, -ātum
Capture, I = capiō, -ere, cēpī, captum
Carry on, I = gerō, -ere, gessī, gestum
Carry, I = portō, -āre, -āvī, -ātum
Catch sight of, I = cōnspiciō, -ere, cōnspexī,
    cōnspectum
Chance, by = forte
Children = līberī, -ōrum, m. pl.
Choose, I = legō, legere, lēgī, lectum
Citizen = cīvis, cīvis, c.
City = urbs, urbis, f.
Clear = clārus, -a, -um
Collect, I = colligō, -ere, collēgī, collēctum
Come, I = veniō, venīre, vēnī, ventum
Companion = comes, comitis, c.; socius, -iī, m.
Concerning = dē + abl.
Conquer, I = vincō, -ere, vīcī, victum
Country, fatherland = patria, -ae, f.
Courage = virtūs, virtūtis, f.
Crowd = turba, -ae, f.
Cruel = crūdēlis, -e
Danger = perīculum, perīculī, n.
Daughter = fīlia, -ae, f.
Dead = mortuus, -a, -um
Dear = cārus, -a, -um
Death = mors, mortis, f.
Decide, I = cōnstituō, -ere, cōnstituī, cōnstitūtum
Deep = altus, -a, -um
Defend, I = dēfendō, -ere, dēfendī, dēfēnsum
Delay = mōra, -ae, f.
Depart, I = discēdō, -ere, discessī, discessum
Destroy, I = dēleō, -ēre, dēlēvī, dēlētum
Die, I = pereō, -īre, -iī, -itum
Difficult = difficilis, -e
Do not… = nōlī/nōlīte (+ infin.)
Do, I = faciō, -ere, fēcī, factum

Down from = dē + abl.
Drink, I = bibō, bibere, bibī
Easy = facilis, -e
Eat, I = cōnsūmō, -ere, cōnsūmpsī, cōnsūmptum
Eight = octo
Eighteen = duodēvīgintī
Eighth = octāvus, -a, -um
Eleven = ūndecim
Enemy = hostis, hostis, c. (usually used in plural)
Enter, I = intrō, -āre, -āvī, -ātum
Escape, I = effugiō, -ere, effūgī
Even, also = etiam
Every = omnis, -e
Famous = clārus, -a, -um; nōtus, -a, -um
Farmer = agricola, -ae, m.
Father = pater, patris, m.
Fatherland = patria, -ae, f.
Fear, I = timeō, -ēre, timuī
Few = paucī, -ae, -a
Field = ager, agrī, m.
Fifteen = quīndecim
Fifth = quīntus, -a, -um
Fight, I = pugnō, -āre, -āvī, -ātum
Find, I = inveniō, -īre, invēnī, inventum
First = prīmus, -a, -um
Five = quīnque
Flee, I = fugiō, -ere, fūgī, fugitum
Food = cibus, cibī, m.
For = nam
For a long time = diū
Forces = cōpiae, -ārum, f. pl.
Fortunate = fēlīx, fēlīcis
Four = quattuor
Fourteen = quattuordecim
Fourth = quārtus, -a, -um
Free, I = līberō, -āre, -āvī, -ātum
Friend = amīcus, amīcī, m.
Frighten, I = terreō, -ēre, terruī, territum
Frightened = perterritus, -a, -um
From = ā/ab + abl.
Gift = dōnum, -ī, n.
Girl = puella, -ae, f.
Give, I = dō, dāre, dedī, dātum
Go, I = eō, īre, iī/īvī, itum
Go across, I = trānseō, -īre, -iī, -itum
Go back, I = redeō, -īre, -iī, -itum
Go in, I = ineō, inīre, iniī, initum
Go out, I = exeō, exīre, exiī, exitum
God = deus, deī, m.

Goddess = dea, -ae, f.
Gold = aurum, -ī, n.
Good = bonus, -a, -um
Great = magnus, -a, -um
Greatly = magnopere
Greek = Graecus, -a, -um
Greet, I = salūtō, -āre, -āvī, -ātum
Ground = terra, -ae, f.
Hand over, I = trādō, -ere, trādidī, trāditum
Happy = laetus, -a, -um
Have, I = habeō, -ēre, habuī, habitum
Hear, I = audiō, audīre, audīvī, audītum
Help = auxilium, -iī, n.
Her (own) = suus, -a, -um
Here = hīc
Herself (reflexive) = sē
High = altus, -a, -um
Himself (reflexive) = sē
His (own) = suus, -a, -um
Hold, I = teneō, -ēre, tenuī, tentum
Horse = equus, equī, m.
How = quam
However = autem; tamen
Huge = ingēns, ingentis
Hurry, I = festīnō, -āre, -āvī, -ātum
Husband = coniūnx, coniugis, c.
I = egŏ
Immediately = statim
In = in + abl.
In front of = prō + abl.
In vain = frūstrā
Inhabitant = incola, -ae, c.
Into = in + acc.
Island = īnsula, -ae, f.
Its (own) = suus, -a, -um
Itself (reflexive) = sē
Journey = iter, itineris, n.
Kill, I = necō, -āre, -āvī, -ātum; occīdō, -ere, occīdī, occīsum
King = rēx, rēgis, m.
Land = terra, -ae, f.
Laugh, I = rīdeō, -ēre, rīsī, rīsum
Lead, I = dūcō, dūcere, dūxī, ductum
Lead back, I = redūcō, -ere, redūxī, reductum
Leader = dux, ducis, m.
Light = lūx, lūcis, f.
Like, I = amō, -āre, -āvī, -ātum
Listen (to), I = audiō, audīre, audīvī, audītum
Little = parvus, -a, -um

Live (in), I = habitō, -āre, -āvī, -ātum
Long = longus, -a, -um
Lord = dominus, dominī, m.
Love, I = amō, -āre, -āvī, -ātum
Make, I = faciō, -ere, fēcī, factum
Man (human) = homō, hominis, m.
Man (as opposed to woman) = vir, virī, m.
Many = multus, -a, -um
Master, lord = dominus, dominī, m.
Master, teacher = magister, magistrī, m.
Messenger = nūntius, nūntiī, m.
Middle = medius, -a, -um
Miserable = miser, misera, miserum
Moreover = autem
Mother = māter, mātris, f.
Mountain = mōns, montis, m.
Move, I = moveō, -ēre, mōvī, mōtum
Much = multus, -a, -um
Name = nōmen, nōminis, n.
Near = prope + acc.
Never = numquam
New = novus, -a, -um
Nine = novem
Nineteen = ūndēvīgintī
Ninth = nōnus, -a, -um
No one = nēmō, nūllius, c.
Noble = nōbilis, -e
Not = nōn
Nothing = nihil
Now = iam
Now = nunc
Often = saepe
Old man = senex, senis, m.
On = in + abl.
On account of = propter + acc.
On behalf of = prō + abl.
On to = in + acc.
Once upon a time = ōlim
One = ūnus
Order, I = iubeō, -ēre, iussī, iussum
Others = cēterī, -ae, -a
Ought, I = dēbeō, -ēre, dēbuī, dēbitum
Our = noster, nostra, nostrum
Out of = ē/ex + abl.
Over = super + acc.
Overcome, I = superō, -āre, -āvī, -ātum
Owe, I = dēbeō, -ēre, dēbuī, dēbitum
Parent = parēns, parentis, c.
Part = pars, partis, f.

Perish, I = pereō, -īre, -iī, -itum
Place = locus, -ī, m.
Place, I = pōnō, -ere, posuī, positum
Play, I = lūdō, -ere, lūsī, lūsum
Poet = poēta, -ae, m.
Praise, I = laudō, -āre, -āvī, -ātum
Prepare, I = parō, -āre, -āvī, -ātum
Present, I am = adsum, adesse, adfuī
Punish, I = pūniō, -īre, pūnīvī, pūnītum
Queen = rēgīna, -ae, f.
Quickly = celeriter
Read, I = legō, legere, lēgī, lectum
Receive, I = accipiō, -ere, accēpī, acceptum
Remain, I = maneō, -ēre, mānsī, mānsum
Report, I = nūntiō, -āre, -āvī, -ātum
Rest, the = cēterī, -ae, -a
River = flūmen, flūminis, n.
Road = via, -ae, f.
Roman = Rōmānus, -a, -um
Rule, I = regō, regere, rēxī, rēctum
Run, I = currō, currere, cucurrī, cursum
Rush, I = ruō, -ere, ruī, rutum
Sacred = sacer, sacra, sacrum
Sad = trīstis, -e
Safe = tūtus, -a, -um
Sail, I = nāvigō, -āre, -āvī, -ātum
Sailor = nauta, -ae, m.
Savage = saevus, -a, -um
Save, I = servō, -āre, -āvī, -ātum
Say, I = dīcō, dīcere, dīxī, dictum
Say, they (quoting direct speech) = inquiunt
Says, he/she (quoting direct speech) = inquit
Sea = mare, maris, n.
Second = secundus, -a, -um
See, I = videō, -ēre, vīdī, vīsum
Seize (a place), I = occupō, -āre, -āvī, -ātum
Send, I = mittō, mittere, mīsī, missum
Seven = septem
Seventeen = septendecim
Seventh = septimus, -a, -um
Shield = scūtum, scūtī, n.
Ship = nāvis, nāvis, f.
Shout = clāmor, clāmōris, m.
Shout, I = clāmō, -āre, -āvī, -ātum
Show, I = ostendō, -ere, ostendī, ostentum
Sing, I = cantō, -āre, -āvī, -ātum
Sister = soror, sorōris, f.
Six = sex
Sixteen = sēdecim

Sixth = sextus, -a, -um
Sky = caelum, -ī, n.
Slave = servus, servī, m.
Slave-girl = ancilla, -ae, f.
Sleep, I = dormiō, -īre, -īvī, -ītum
Small = parvus, -a, -um
So, thus = sīc
Soldier = mīles, mīlitis, m.
Son = fīlius, fīliī, m.
Soon = mox
Spear = hasta, -ae, f.
Stand, I = stō, -āre, stetī, stătum
Street = via, -ae, f.
Strong = fortis, -e; validus, -a, -um
Suddenly = subitō
Surely... = nōnne? (introduces a question expecting
    the answer 'yes')
Surely ... not = num? (introduces a question
    expecting the answer 'no')
Sword = gladius, gladiī, m.
Take, I = capiō, -ere, cēpī, captum
Tell, I = nārrō, -āre, -āvī, -ātum
Temple = templum, templī, n.
Ten = decem
Tenth = decimus, -a, -um
Terrified = perterritus, -a, -um
Terrify, I = terreō, -ēre, terruī, territum
That (over there) = ille, illa, illud
That (near me) = is, ea, id
Their (own) = suus, -a, -um
Themselves (reflexive) = sē
Then = deinde; tum
There = ibi
Therefore = igitur; itaque
Third = tertius, -a, -um
Thirteen = tredecim
This = hic, haec, hoc
Three = trēs
Through = per + acc.
Throw, I = iaciō, -ere, iēcī, iactum
Thus = sīc
Tired = fessus, -a, -um
To (towards) = ad + acc.
Tomorrow = crās
Towards = ad + acc.

Town = oppidum, oppidī, n.
Twelve = duodecim
Twenty = vīgintī
Two = duŏ
Under = sub + abl.
Unhappy = miser, misera, miserum
Voice = vōx, vōcis, f.
Wait for, I = exspectō, -āre, -āvī, -ātum
Wall = mūrus, mūrī, m.
Wander, I = errō, -āre, -āvī, -ātum
Want, I = cupiō, -ere, cupīvī, cupītum
War = bellum, bellī, n.
Warn, I = moneō, -ēre, monuī, monitum
Watch, I = spectō, -āre, -āvī, -ātum
Water = aqua, -ae, f.
Wave = unda, -ae, f.
We = nōs
Weapons = arma, -ōrum, n. pl.
Wear = gerō, -ere, gessī, gestum
Well = bene
Well-known = nōtus, -a, -um
What? = quid?
When = ubi
Where? = ubi?
Who? = quis?
Why? = cūr?
Wife = coniūnx, coniugis, c.; uxor, uxōris, f.
Wind = ventus, -ī, m.
Wine = vīnum, -ī, n.
Wise = sapiēns, sapientis
With (together with) = cum + abl.
Without = sine + abl.
Woman = fēmina, -ae, f.; mulier, mulieris, f.
Word = verbum, verbī, n.
Work, I = labōrō, -āre, -āvī, -ātum
Wound = vulnus, vulneris, n.
Wound, I = vulnerō, -āre, -āvī, -ātum
Wretched = miser, misera, miserum
Write, I = scrībō, -ere, scrīpsī, scriptum
Yesterday = herī
You (pl.) = vōs
You (sing.) = tū
Young man = iuvenis, iuvenis, c.
Your (of you (pl.)) = vester, vestra, vestrum
Your (of you (sing.)) = tuus, -a, -um

Index